COUNTY
CLARE
its towns and villages

COUNTY CLARE

its towns and villages

Arthur Flynn

TEMPUS

This book is dedicated to Luke

Frontispiece: Goldnight Castle

First published 2004

Tempus Publishing Limited
The Mill, Brimscombe Port,
Stroud, Gloucestershire, GL5 2QG
www.tempus-publishing.com

British Library Cataloguing in Publication Data.
A catalogue record for this book is available from the British Library.

ISBN 0 7524 3289 3

Typesetting and origination by Tempus Publishing Limited.
Printed in Great Britain.

Contents

Acknowledgements

I would like to thank the following for their assistance in the preparation of this book.

Michael Kelleher, Margaret Neylon, Paddy Kelly, Gerry Connolly, Noel Rowsome, Garrett Flynn, Clare Champion, John Leonard, Shannon Development, Clare County Library, GAA Clare, National Library of Ireland, John Horgan, Bunratty Castle, Trinity College Library, Dublin, Ennis Tourist Office and, especially, Margret Field for photographs and Peter Beirne of Clare Local Studies Library.

Preface

County Clare is situated mid-way along the west coast, in the province of Munster and covers an area of approximately 1,325 square miles. This large county extends from Galway Bay in the north, across the lunar landscape of the Burren to Lough Derg, with the Atlantic Ocean forming its rugged western boundary. The southern area is bordered by the lower sections of the River Shannon. The entire coastline is relatively bare and shaped by cliffs that offer little shelter to ships and vessels between its southern corner, at Loop Head, and Galway Bay that lies beyond its northern boundary at Black Head.

The county could almost be termed a peninsula as the bulk of its boundary is sea, river and lake. The River Shannon serves as a natural divide separating it from the neighbouring counties of Kerry, Limerick and Tipperary.

Off the coastline there are a series of islands including Mutton Island, Scattery Island, Graigue Island, Crab Island, Canon Island, Horse Island, Green Island, Oilean na Leime, Fergus Island and Inishmurray and off the north Clare coast the Aran Islands of Inishmore, Inishmaan and Inisheer. The River Shannon enters the Atlantic Ocean between Loop Head and Kerry Head. The landscapes of Clare contrast dramatically with the unique form of the Burren, to beaches, towering cliffs, lakes and rivers. To the north-west the rugged coast road rises to 700 feet above the sea culminating with the spectacular Cliffs of Moher. One of the most visited areas is the astonishing limestone district called the Burren with its array of caves, rare flora, rock formations and underground streams. The Poulnagollum-Pollelva complex is the largest cave network in the Burren. A visit to Aillwee Cave will give the traveller of to day a glimpse into a world that was formed millions of years ago.

County Clare, officially established in the sixteenth century, has many varied and contrasting dimensions. The county is rich in antiquity and archaeological remains ranging from earthen and stone forts dating to pre-Celtic times and megalithic tombs to stone crosses bearing testimony to the early inhabitants. The remains of many ancient churches and ecclesiastical sites dating to the sixth century are evident throughout north Clare. There are approximately five round towers and 200 castles scattered throughout the county, some of which, like Bunratty and

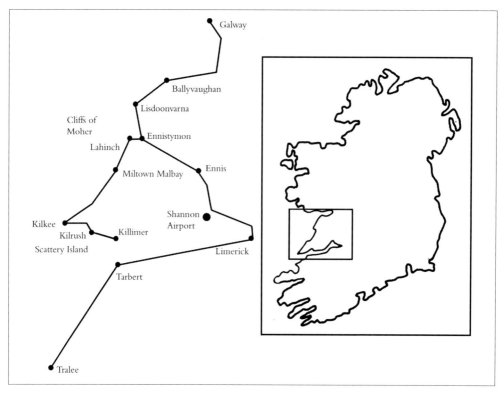

Map of West of Ireland showing the roads into and out of County Clare

Knappogue, now host Medieval Banquets. From the eighth century the main families were the O'Briens, O'Deas, O'Loughlins, McNamaras and MacMahons, who fought off invaders and also engaged in skirmishes among themselves.

The county offers many opportunities for social activities particularly swimming, fishing and boating.

In this book I have divided the county into several broad areas: 1. West Clare: extending from Ballyvaughan to the Burren, along the coast past to the Cliffs of Moher and onto Lahinch and Kilrush. 2. Mid-Clare: extending from Bunratty to Shannon onto Ennis and Corofin. 3. East Clare: extending from Whitegate to Mountshannon to Killaloe and Sixmilebridge. In each section I have given a short history of each town and village and any famous people or events associated with the area.

The attractions of County Clare are many: its rich cultural and historical past; unspoilt beaches; breathtaking views from the Cliffs of Moher; rounds of golf on the county's many fine courses; its strong traditional music culture; the craic in Lisdoonvara; romantic strolls on Bishop's Quarter Beach; exploring the amazing landscapes of the Burren; numerous walking trials and boat trips on Lough Derg.

From the early 1990s the Mullaghmore area of the Burren was the centre of a major controversy when the area was designated to become a national park and an interpretative centre. There was a country-wide reaction and the Burren Action Group campaigned for four years against the site until finally the government abandoned the project.

The largest and most important towns in the county are Ennis, Kilrush, Ennistymon, Kilkee, Lisdoonvarna, Miltown Malbay, Corofin, Ballyvaughan and Lahinch. Ennis is the administration capital with the Clare County offices located there. For those seeking addition information there is an extensive Local Studies section in Clare County Library with a very attentive staff.

Many prominent figures have had connections with the county including Brian Boru, Daniel O'Connell, Eamon de Valera, Charles Stewart Parnell, Biddy Early and Patrick Hillery. The county has also produced some outstanding painters, poets and writers.

Clare is referred to as the Banner County, a title that is believed to have emerged when crowds turned out waving banners to greet such politicians as Daniel O'Connell, Charles Stewart Parnell and Eamon de Valera.

History of County Clare

According to legend County Clare takes its name from a plank, as the Irish form An Clar, 'A Plank' or 'Board' or 'A Level Place,' as one of its translations implies. It is believed that at Clarecastle a plank was placed across the River Fergus to serve as a bridge. In 1248 King Henry II granted lands to the Norman knight, Robert de Muscegros at this strategic location and he built a bridge and castle there.

At the end of the Ice Age, Mesolithic man came to Ireland, and traces of Mesolithic culture have been discovered along the Clare coast. The Neolithic, or later Stone Age, culture began in Ireland around 6,500 years ago, leaving passage graves around the Burren area. Stone Age people first arrived on Clare's isolated coastline over 5,000 years ago. A Celtic tribe, known as Corcu Modruad, settled in the northern part of Clare approximately 2,000 years ago. According to the scholar, Eugene O'Curry, a large monument known as Carn Connachtach was the inauguration area of the chieftains of Corcu Modruad.

Signs of early life in the Burren are evident in the many Stone Age burial monuments such as Gleninsheen wedge tomb and Poulnabrone Dolmen. The many ringforts scattered throughout the Burren signify a later period of habitation as with Ballykinvarga and Cahercommaun.

Bronze Age man was to leave mine workings, traces of houses and fields, assembly places, copper and bronze tools and weapons, rock carvings and great wedge tombs dotted across the county. Dating from about 500 BC old roads, field systems, stone and promontory forts and ring or eastern forts can be seen. Another delight of the Burren is the diverse range of flora and fauna that grow here in such abundance although they require vastly different climates.

There also remains an extraordinary body of legends of Irish legends from this period that became the basis of much of early Irish literature for the next 2,000 years.

In certain sectors of County Clare there are little signs of early settlements or human habitation. One such area is the Loop Head district where there is little evidence except where standing stones and ring barrows have been discovered. Over fifty per cent of the archaeological sites of Clare are in the area of the Burren.

Drumcliffe.

Bronze Age man constantly found himself under attack and as a means of defence some built their homes on a lake. One of the best known of these dwellings was the crannog, a simple structure made from reeds, wattles and mud. Close by there was a communal cooking area known as a fulacht fiadh where families would cook meat on a spit. A number of such places have been discovered throughout Clare. In 1852 two crannogs were exposed at Ballyalla and Drumcliffe when the lake level dropped. The best example of this form of life can be seen at Craggaunowen, near Quin. Craggaunowen Castle was restored and a Bronze Age crannog has been created that includes a ring fort, dwellings and an outdoor cooking area.

Clare formed the central portion of the old Kingdom of Thomond and when in the sixteenth century the earldom of Thomond was established its area represented mostly the present County Clare. The earliest inhabitants of the county are part of pre-history and there is little information available of their activities. The Book of Invasion or Leabhar Gabhala, a collection of accounts of mythological groups, connect Clare with the Fir Bolg. They settled in the west of Ireland and are associated with Magh Adhair in Clare, Lough Cultra in Galway and Dun Aongus in the Aran Islands.

One of the first names to feature in the history of Clare was Cas, a contemporary of Saint Patrick in the fifth century. Cas was a member of the Munster Royal family and his descendant's territory extended from Limerick to Cashel. Other saints associated with the early history of Clare are Saint Flannan of Killaloe and Saint Senan of Scattery Island.

By the mid-tenth century an aggressive new power emerged in Munster. This was the Dalg Cais (tribe of Cas) or Dalcassins, who had settled along the lower Shannon and begun to expand their territory across the river into Clare. They established a small chiefdom in east Clare and their leader Mathgamain also captured the kingship of Cashel from the Eoganachta in 964. Soon afterwards he defeated the Vikings at Limerick at the battle of Sulchoid and sacked the city.

In 950, an uncle of Brian Boroime (Boru), Lachtna, established a stronghold at Crag Liath, north of Killaloe, County Clare. He withstood the advance of the Vikings. His nephew, Mathgamain, succeeded him but was killed in 976 and his second nephew, Brian Boru, took control. Brian and Mahon successfully extended their boundaries still further and organised a defensive campaign against the Vikings at Scattery Island and Limerick. Within a short period Brian Boru succeeded in forcing each clan to submit and he was acknowledged as King of Cashel. By 984 Brian was so powerful that he had become king of the whole south of Ireland combining Munster, Leinster and Ossory.

A decisive event was the Battle of Glen Mama in 999 at which Brian Boru defeated the king of Leinster and the Dublin Vikings, after which he plundered the city. Three years later Mael Sechnaill, without a battle, surrendered to him at Tara and Brian became High King of Ireland. Over the next twelve years Brian had to suppress dissident northern kings but the strongest resistance came from the kingdom of Leinster. Simultaneously with maintaining national control Brian built a vast empire in Clare. He erected Kincora, his royal residence and rebuilt the churches of Killaloe and Inis Cealtra that had been destroyed by the Vikings. He saw the potential of the Shannon and soon had 300 boats on Lough Derg. It was possible to sail up to Carrick-on-Shannon after the boats had been carried overland at Ardnacrusha Falls. Brian also initiated the building of roads and bridges.

In 1014, the king of Leinster, Mael Morda joined with the Vikings of Dublin in a great show of strength at Clontarf and engaged Brian Boru and his force on Good Friday in the Battle of Clontarf. The Irish had a decisive victory that saw the end of Viking dominance in Ireland. Following the battle, a Viking named Broder killed Brian Boru in his tent. Brian's son, Murrough, was also killed.

Prior to the tenth century not every individual had a surname but Brian Boru made it compulsory that everybody was to have a surname. His own descendants chose his name as a form of their own. This move was to firmly establish the name O'Brien for many centuries as a formidable name in the history of County Clare. Brian Boru is reputed to have been married four times and his many offspring formed branches of the O'Brien clan.

In a relatively short span of time the territory of the O'Briens shrank to the area of Thomond (north Munster) and hostilities continued against the O'Connors of Connacht. Around this period the O'Brien clan split into several different

Mucknish castle, Ballyvaughan, c. 1910.

branches. The main place of inauguration for the O'Briens as princes and kings of Thomond, was at Tulla, County Clare. Their motto was 'Lamb Laidir An Uachdar' or 'The Strong Hand Uppermost.' Their coat-of-arms bore three lions that were on the standard of Brian Boru and carried by his troops at the Battle of Clontarf. In 1157 the King of Thomond, Turlough O'Brien, made an incursion into south Munster to regain his land. In 1169 Dermot MacMurrough and the Anglo-Normans arrived in Ireland and were seen by Donal Mor O'Brien as allies in his feud with the High King of Ireland, Rory O'Connor. Donal swore allegiance to King Henry II but realised his folly and took up arms against the Normans. Despite valiant efforts the Normans failed to capture a strong base in Clare.

In 1248 King Henry III made grants of land to the Norman knight, Robert de Muscegros at an annual rent of £30. De Muscegros built two castles, one at Clare Castle and one at Bunratty, two strategic locations blocking the entrance to the River Fergus and Bunratty. Clare Castle blocked access to Clonroad, stronghold of the O'Briens. When Conor O'Brien died, his successor, Brian Rua, destroyed Clare Castle and re-established the O'Briens in the territory of Tradraige. This resulted in De Muscegros surrendering his land to the king, who in 1276 granted Bunratty castle and its lands to Thomas de Clare, a younger son of the Earl of Gloucester. When Turlough O'Brien ousted Brian Rua as King of Thomond, Brian Rua asked de Clare for assistance and they entered an agreement that the Normans would only colonise land east of the Quin River. Thomas de Clare married Maurice Fitzmaurice's daughter and was granted the territory of Thomond.

Another de Clare, Richard, plundered the area and in 1318 was defeated at the Battle of Dysert O'Dea. Following the battle the de Clares were expelled and the English did not re-emerge in the county for over two centuries.

In the mid-fourteenth century there was a great revival in Gaelic institutions and customs. From this period many accounts were written by lawyers for the schools of law on old Irish law tracts. One of the most prestigious of these was the famous school of the Davorens of County Clare. The Book of Ballymore also dates from this period and was a great volume of Irish learning, verse and story. The Anglo-Irish gentry patronised the Gaelic men of letters and without their support the scholars and poets would have found it difficult to survive.

In later years the O'Briens gained prominence as the Earls of Inchiquin, Barons of Clare and Marquises of Thomond. Some of the O'Briens became distinguished officers in the Irish brigades who fought in the service of France under the titles of Earls of Clare and Counts of Thomond.

Ballinalacken castle, c. 1910.

The quiet village of Broadford.

In 1534 when King Henry VIII came to the throne, royal dominance was reasserted in Clare. It was not until 1541 that the English gained total control in Clare. In 1559 at Spancill Hill, County Clare, Earl Conor and his ally, the Earl of Desmond, were defeated by the Dalcassian clans. At this time Tadgh O'Brien was appointed High Sheriff of Clare. This was the first occasion in which the term County Clare was used referring to the land mass.

From the thirteenth century the Crowd made several unsuccessful attempts to 'shire' Clare but the O'Briens were the main reason for the delay. In the late 1560s Conor O'Brien would not surrender his lands in Clarecastle to Queen Elizabeth I and continued to operate hit and run raids on English forces and the property of the Crown. Finally Conor O'Brien reached a compromise with the Crown and in 1569 the province of Connaught was divided into four counties Galway, Mayo, Sligo and Clare. Morrough O'Brien became Earl of Thomond when it was separated from Munster and placed under the President of Connacht. Conor O'Brien insisted that Clare should be part of Munster and eventually it reverted back to that status. In 1569 the first Protestant Bishop of Clare was appointed. During the sixteenth century the natives of Clare were less interested in titles or grants so long as their chief was in control. Clare did not officially become a county until 1576.

Ennis, the principal town of County Clare was to develop naturally on a ridge over the River Fergus at the junction of the Galway and Limerick roads. There were no walls to the town as it was primarily an island. In 1609 a royal grant permitted a weekly market to be held in the town. Under English law Irish chieftains could take out patents on markets and fairs and extract income. With its prime location beside the friary and on the river, boats could travel upriver to trade and barter in farm produce, hides and wool. The humble dwellings of the residents expanded outwards from this focal point.

The Spanish Armada featured in some important events in the history of County Clare that are commemorated in the name Spanish Point. In 1588 the Armada, sent by King Philip II to invade England fought a series of running battles with the British fleet. In September the vessels headed north around Scotland and down the west coast of Ireland en route back to Spain but they were battered by storms and sought refuge in sheltered inlets. Many of the vessels were wrecked off the coast of Clare with the survivors receiving a variety of fates. One of the ships broke up on a reef known as Rinn Dubh, south of Doolin Pier.

There were reports of over 700 sailors being drowned and almost 200 taken prisoner. The High Sheriff of Clare, Boetius MacClancy ordered that the prisoners be brought to Doonagore Castle, near Doolin. Some were killed while others were transferred to the castle. A bloody episode in Clare's history was then enacted in September 1588 when MacClancy sentenced all the prisoners to death and there were mass hangings of Spanish sailors on the Hill of the Hanging. The prisoners were buried in an unmarked grave on the beach. Other Spanish ships sought refuge on Scattery Island and remained there until the storm abated. One of their ships was so badly damaged that the crew burned it rather than let it fall into the hands of the Irish. The remaining Spanish ships made good their escape and continued their journey back to Spain. Locals along the coast were to have a bumper time as they plundered the wreckage of the ships as it was washed up on the rocks and beach.

In the Rebellion of 1641 the Earl of Thomond fought on the British side while other branches of the O'Brien and the McNamara clans took the Catholic side and participated in the Confederation of Kilkenny. The war lasted from 1641 to 1654, leaving the country in a deplorable state. When civil war broke out in England, the Earl of Thomond, supported King Charles I but in 1646 he reluctantly allowed a parliamentary garrison to take Bunratty castle. They established a camp at this strategic location. Shortly afterwards the castle was recaptured by the Confederation but fell to General Ireton in the Cromwellian push. The native Irish clans joined together to oppose Ireton.

In 1650 the new Lord Lieutenant, Oliver Cromwell set about implementing his campaign of transforming the nature of the landed aristocracy in Ireland. He engaged in widespread slaughter and made his decree 'To Hell or to Connaught' on hearing that a large part of Clare had 'no trees from which to hang a man, nor enough water to drown him, nor enough soil to bury him.' Cromwell declared it the ideal place to banish the rebellious Irish and his force did much damage in Clare as most of the landlords supported the royalists. Castles and estates were attacked and Catholic landowners were dispossessed and their lands were granted to Protestants. Churches and monasteries were destroyed, their property confiscated and the monks and priests went into hiding.

For the next two centuries Clare was to be devastated by wars and the effects of famine. There was a dramatic reduction in the population of the county due to death and emigration.

Baron Inchiquin resisted the parliament forces but was defeated and took refuge in France. In the 1660s, with the Restoration of the monarchy, Charles II granted Baron Inchiquin the presidency of Munster. With the Restoration many families felt that their property would be returned but this did not become a reality. Catholics had to conform to the established (Anglican) Church if they hoped to regain their land.

In 1689-1690 Clare was to endure further hardship under the reign of James II that ended in defeat for him and the Irish cause. Sir Donough O'Brien of Dromoland and Leamaneh castles, and high-sheriff of the county supported James during this period.

From the mid-seventeenth century thousands of Irishmen, including many from Clare, joined regiments of the English army while others joined armies throughout Europe that were at war with England. These men became known as the Wild Geese, a term attributed to them by the captains of ships that transported them to fight against England.

Viscount Clare, another O'Brien, formed a regiment of horse soldiers that became known as 'Clare's Dragoons.' They were defeated in the Battle of the Boyne but fought many successful campaigns on European battlefields. The Third Viscount Clare, Daniel O'Brien, founded the Infantry Regiment that later became known as the Regiment of Clare. The estates of William O'Brien, Earl of Inchiquin, were confiscated by James II but were later restored by William III. The Earl of Inchiquin and his descendants played a pivotal role in the Protestant ascendancy that was to shape and influence Irish society in the eighteenth and nineteenth centuries.

The implementation of the Penal Laws was to prove another period of oppression for the people of Clare. The laws imposed by Parliament were to restrict the activities of Catholics and to secure the privileged position of the Church of Ireland, the established church. Under Queen Anne a law was passed whereby all Catholic clergy had to be registered. Each priest had to provide two

An abandoned traditional cottage.

securities of £50 each to ensure their good behaviour. The clergy of County Clare were fortunate in that there were many Catholic landlords possessing property and wealth who could sponsor them. Each of the dioceses including Killaloe, Ennis and Kilfenora set up registration for their priests. The State of Popery in Ireland recorded that in 1729 there were only seven priests in the diocese of Kilfenora. In some areas where these laws were enforced over zealously mass houses were set up and some masses were said in secluded places, old houses and at mass rocks. Dublin castle implemented a policy of rewarding informers for reporting unregistered priests.

As the Penal Laws were eased and gradually phased out an organisation called the Whiteboys was established in Munster in 1761. This was a blanket name for different Catholic secret societies that were engaged in violent disturbances relating to resentment at taxes and charges from arable to dairy farming and sectarianism. They also protested about the amounts of the tithes that were to be contributed to the Established Church. Around this period most of the poor children attended hedge schools. Here they were given a basic education of the 'Three Rs': reading, writing and arithmetic. The teachers were not paid and depended on the generosity of donations from the families.

In response to the growing unrest throughout the country and the possibility of a French invasion, a militia act for Ireland was passed in 1793. Since the 1770s there had been a volunteer force but this had proved ineffective and was disorganised. The new bill gave powers for the creation of a strong militia force in every county throughout the country. The Clare militia was founded in 1793 and could create up to seven companies. The headquarters for the militia was Clarecastle where they paraded regularly. From the outset it was policy for the militia not to be stationed in their own county for fear of fraternisation with the enemy. Initially the Clare militia was based in Louth and later, in Waterford.

In 1794 the Society of the United Irishmen was established with the goal of achieving economic and political independence for Ireland. The United Irishmen of Munster, with a force of approximately 100,000, men were to have taken part in the 1798 Rising but this was aborted with the arrest of many of their leaders in the province. Recruitment in Clare was keen, particularly in the larger towns. Many of the volunteers arrested in Clare were tortured, jailed and others were transported to Australia, West Indies and America. There were frequent public floggings in Ennis as an example to others who might support the United Irishmen. Even members of the Catholic clergy strongly denounced the activities of other priests who supported the organisation. When news reached Clare that a French fleet had landed at Killala Bay the volunteers were ready to rise but it was a false alarm as the fleet had only sought shelter from a storm. The 1798 Rebellion was mainly concentrated in the Wicklow/Wexford area and Clare did not become involved.

One of the people to have greatest impact on County Clare was the Kerry Catholic landlord, Daniel O'Connell, known as the Liberator. From the early nineteenth century he was a prominent voice against the Act of Union. His Catholic Association movement rallied the ordinary people behind him. In 1828 the leading Clare figure, Charles O'Gorman Mahon from Ennis encouraged Daniel O'Connell to run as a candidate in Clare against the sitting member of parliament, Vesey Fitzgerald. Fitzgerald was a strong candidate who had held the seat for ten years and had a post in the British cabinet. At that period a Catholic could not sit in Parliament but they were eligible to go forward as a candidate. Big farmers and the gentry supported Fitzgerald. Many of the Catholic tenants and small farmers were under threat of eviction if they voted for O'Connell but they still backed him en masse. Priests canvassed their congregations and led the people in disciplined groups to the polling booths to vote for O'Connell. In this famous election the people of Clare returned Daniel O'Connell to the British Parliament with 2,057 votes against 982 for Fitzgerald. Although Catholic Emancipation was granted the following year Catholics were still committed to paying tithes to the Established Church. It was during this period that Clare earned the title 'The Banner County.'

In the early 1830s in the village of Rathlahine, close to Newmarket-on-Fergus, a secret organisation known as the Terry Alts caused land agitation. These were gangs of landless labourers and small tenant farmers who resented the landlords and murdered the steward of the large landlord, John Scott Vandeleur of Rathlaheen House. Following the murder, Vandeleur sought to find a solution to the problem and invited Edward Craig, an expert in the co-operative movement, to establish a co-op in Clare. The result was the Ralahine Agricultural and Manufacturing Co-operative Association on Vandeleur's estate. Members were admitted to the co-operative on strict terms with rates of pay and prices set for farm produce. Schooling and medical care was provided for their families. The co-operative proved hugely successful but its activities were short-lived as Vandeleur was declared bankrupt and the co-operative ceased to operate.

With an increasing level of poverty throughout Ireland the Poor Relief (Ireland) Act (1838) was introduced to try and ease the situation. Under the Act the country was divided into 130 Poor Law 'unions' or groups of parishes, each centred on a market town. Each union was self-sufficient and had to provide for its own poor by means of a levy on all property and to build its own workhouse. Irish landlords in the main funded the operation. Ennis had the largest workhouse with four auxiliary ones in the town and two more in Clarecastle that could accommodate over 5,000 people.

Other workhouses were built in the larger towns throughout Clare such as Scarriff, Kilrush, Ennistymon and Ballyvaughan. Shortly after opening their doors they were all filled to capacity and set about turning people away. Some paupers, too weak to return home, died outside the walls. In addition to the workhouse, the authorities organised a relief scheme to assist the poor. These schemes involved road-widening, clearing scrubland and wall-building. Kilrush was one of the most popular workhouses and there were many famine relief schemes in the area. Some peasants even travelled by boat to seek work on the schemes. In December 1849 a ferry returning from Kilrush sank in Poulnasherry Bay with the loss of all thirty-four on board. They were all paupers from Loop Head who had travelled to the Kilrush workhouse to seek admission or get onto work schemes. Their bodies were washed up on the shoreline. The following year in another sea tragedy in the area nineteen cattle jobbers were also drowned.

Fortunately the Poor Law scheme was in operation before the potato blight affected the crop of 1845. Prior to this the scheme had assisted the poor but with the famine a wider section of society felt its effects. Shortage of food was a regular occurrence for many families but not to the degree of the Great Famine of 1845-49 that was to become one of the worst human catastrophes in the country's history.

On the coast the poor were forced to eat sea-grass, periwinkles and limpets. Inland, starving families resorted to eating nettles, dandelions, watercress and even grass. They set traps for rabbits and any other form of wildlife. All forms of birds were at risk from starving families. Some benevolent landlords set up soup kitchens throughout the county, but some principled peasants would starve rather than become a 'souper'. This was the term applied to people who converted to Protestantism in order to get soup or food. This practice was widespread in Clare when many soup kitchens were disrupted. One such incident occurred at Meelick when the soup kitchen of landlord Delmege was attacked and smashed. From Corofin came reports of similar incidents. There are accounts of turnips, carrots and cabbage being stolen from the fields of farmers.

County Clare fared badly during the famine. In 1841 the population of the county stood at 286,394 but a decade later this figure had been reduced to 212,440. This left an incredible gap of over 73,000 people that either died of disease or starvation or emigrated in a ten-year period. There are many reports of the families of labourers and small farmers dying of starvation at a time when most families lived in a one-roomed mud cabin with poor sanitary conditions.

In the period from 1845-50, 50,000 people died in the county and thousands emigrated to North America, Canada, Australia and Liverpool in search of brighter futures. Some of the clergy and benevolent landlords assisted families to emigrate. One such individual was Col. George Wyndham who helped many peasant families from his estates to emigrate to Canada. Emigration was sadly not always an escape from disaster as on one ship that set out from Kilrush to Canada thirty-seven passengers died from fever before the ship reached its destination.

In 1849 the authorities implemented a new policy ending outdoor relief schemes for able-bodied paupers. Prior to this the Boards of Guardians of many of the workhouses in Clare were closed. Following requests three Clare unions, Scariff, Kilrush and Ennistymon had their boards restored.

The Irish National Land League founded by Charles Stewart Parnell and Michael Davitt aimed to protect tenant's rights and the abolition of landlordism. In one of the most famous speeches of his career Parnell addressed a large gathering of farmers in Ennis. He advised them that if there was to be a land reform passed in the next session of parliament that it would be up to them not to pay unjust rents. 'It will be the measure of your determination not to bid for houses from which others have been evicted, and to use the strong force of public opinion to deter any unjust men amongst yourselves – and there are many such – from bidding for such farms. Any one who transgresses the code should be placed in a 'moral Coventry', shunned by his neighbours 'as if he were a leper of old'.

Under the 1881 Land Law (Ireland) Act tenants were permitted to have their rents fixed for a period of fifteen years. Col. John O'Callaghan of Maryfort was a prosperous landlord and treated his tenants fairly until, that was, 1886. In that year the prices for farm produce fell dramatically and when tenants requested a reduction in rent from O'Callaghan he refused. This resulted in conflict between the tenants and the National League on one side and the landlords on the other. In 1887 twenty-seven families were evicted from O'Callaghan's estate in Bodyke. A major confrontation ensued in which 5,000 people supported the tenants and the events received international coverage. Following protracted negotiations the matter was resolved to the satisfaction of the tenants.

Some of the leading names in Irish politics have had connections with County Clare. The names Daniel O'Connell, Charles Stewart Parnell, Eamon de Valera and Patrick Hillery have become synonymous with politics in the county.

The East Clare by-election of 1917 is another historic date as Eamon de Valera's 5,010 votes defeated Patrick Lynch's 2,035. This was an overwhelming victory for Dev and Sinn Féin. De Valera had been in charge of the Boland's Mills garrison during the 1916 Rising and a death sentence passed on him had been commuted. He was then invited to stand in East Clare where over 200 delegates from East and West Clare attended the Sinn Féin Convention in Ennis that nominated him.

With Sinn Féin's control over local government the British system of justice was supplanted by a form of 'Dail Courts' that were first operated in West Clare and during 1919 and 1920 they spread rapidly.

In de Valera the electors saw the senior surviving commandant of the Easter Rising and realised that a vote for him was not just a vote against the parliamentary party but a vote for 1916. This was de Valera's first parliamentary battle and newly released from prison he took his stand on the Proclamation for which Patrick Pearse and the other leaders had died. In the General Election of 1918 Eamon de Valera was returned unopposed for Clare. By this time he was President of Sinn Féin.

In September 1922 de Valera was given a civil reception on his return to Ennis with thousands lining the street to greet him. De Valera was to retain the Clare seat for forty-two years from 1917-1959 when he won the presidential election against Sean Mac Eoin. Following an impressive career in active politics he became fifth president of Ireland.

Another de Valera, Sile, Eamon's grand-daughter, was to carry the family mantel later when she was elected for Fianna Fáil in Clare. She was appointed Junior Minister for Arts & Heritage, Gaeltacht and the Islands in the 28th Dail in 1997.

In 1925 the Free State government undertook one of the state's most ambitious projects when they diverted the Shannon and built a huge hydro-electric station at Ardnacrusha. The ESB power station became a necessity due to the increasing demand for electricity. The project proved to be an overwhelming success and was lauded internationally. The operation entailed recruiting over

5,000 men, at a period of high unemployment, some of whom walked for many days to the site where the workers were accommodated in a temporary village. Water was diverted via a dam and through a head-race canal that had to be blasted from the rock. In 1929 the power station went into service providing 96 per cent of the country's electricity demand at the time. In 1941 the writer, Sean O'Faolain wrote:

> All this region between Lough Derg and Slieve Aughty and the sea is, physically speaking, lovely in a way that no other part of Ireland is lovely. That is the thing about Clare, which gives it such attraction. It is hard, and barren, and windy, and wild, yet its power to enchant comes from the delicacy and lightness and gentleness of its lyrical moods. Clare is now a shaggy-dressed, hairy-faced, dark-eyed, rough-voiced man of the roads – a drover or a travelling man: now a girl whose natural wildness is constantly forgotten in and overlain by the softness of her temperament. This land full of grey rocks, little lakes, large horizons, seeping dusk, clumped trees, wandering and winding roads, happy green nooks among the stones, rich deposits among the boglands, is the west without the savagery of the west, and the midlands without their sloth and ease.

On 10 March 1968, the leading Fianna Fáil minister, Donagh O'Malley died suddenly while canvassing in the General Election, in Sixmilebridge. Another important politician to feature in the history of County Clare is Dr Patrick Hillery. Dr Hillery was born in Miltown Malbay in 1923. He was educated at the local national school, Rockwell College and University College, Dublin. He became a doctor and in 1951 he was elected TD for West Clare for Fianna Fáil. He represented the constituency until 1953 and served in several ministries. In 1973 he became the Irish Commissioner in the EEC with responsibility for Social Affairs. In 1976 he became the agreed candidate and was installed as the sixth President of Ireland.

Since 1995 there has been a new-found pride within the realms of the GAA when Clare won its first All-Ireland Senior Hurling title since 1914. The famous 'Clare shout' was heard from one end of the county to the other. There has been a long and worthy tradition of Gaelic Games in the county since Michael Cusack of Carron became one of the founding fathers of the Gaelic Athletic Association (GAA) in Hayes' Hotel, Thurles on 1 November 1884. Cusack sent out a call for the people to take the management of athletics into their own hands and 'to promote every form of athletics that is peculiarly Irish, and remove with one sweep everything foreign and iniquitous in the present system.' There is a stand named after Cusack in Croke Park. In 1887 the first County Championship games were played in Clare.

Young supporters celebrating Clare's victory in the All-Ireland, 1999.

For over a century Clare has been a favourite tourist destination with families returning annually to many of the resorts from Lahinch with its huge breakers, Kilkee with its coastal walks and Kilrush with its marina. Throughout the county there are a number of heritage centres offering historical and archaeological information about the heritage and culture of County Clare.

Traditional music and dance have stronger links with County Clare than any other county. The early history of the county reveals a constant shifting of population through migration and invasions, each group bringing its own music and dance. The earliest influences were the Druids, who danced in religious ritual to the oak and the sun. Traces of their circular dances still survive in the ring dances. The Siege of Ennis is a form of dance originating from this era. An assortment of instruments has provided the music down through the years. Formerly the bagpipe was the most popular instrument. In 1601 when the British outlawed pipers and their instruments were destroyed, they made whistles from corn-cobs.

From the late eighteenth-century one of the best-known figures in County Clare was the Dancing Master. He travelled from village to village with a blind fiddler and was paid by the people for teaching their children to dance. The Dancing Master was a flamboyant figure who wore brightly coloured clothes.

Each one had his own district and never moved into the territory of a rival. It was not unknown for a Dancing Master to be kidnapped by the residents of a neighbouring parish. On meeting at fairs or similar events they would challenge each other and hold a dancing contest in public. This sometimes lasted for several hours. A problem the Dancing Masters sometimes encountered was that some of the children did not know their left from their right foot. To overcome this he tied straw or hay to each foot and gave the orders as 'lift hay foot' or 'lift straw foot.'

When crossroads dancing was introduced the clergy took exception to it as an 'occasion of sin' and drove the dancers indoors. This led to the first ceili being held in 1897 that in turn led to the formation of ceili bands. Two of the most famous ceili bands in the country, the award-winning Kilfenora that was established early in the twentieth century and the Tulla, hail from County Clare. In 1973 the Willie Clancy Summer School was initiated in Miltown Malbay to honour the memory of the great master of traditional instruments and accomplished a piper. Since its inception it has been held annually and has developed into one of the major cultural events in the country attracting participants from around the globe. Other well-known musical names to emerge from Clare are Miko, Gus and Packo Russell and Sharon Shannon.

Many songs and dances were not written down but passed from generation to generation. Set-dancing still plays a big part in the social life of the county from sessions in houses to pubs and hotels. Due to its contribution to set-dancing, the Clare Set has become synonymous with the dance countrywide. With its strong musical tradition it is not surprising that over the years Clare has been immortalised in song. Some of the best known ones are: 'Clare's Dragoons', 'The Darling Girl from Clare', 'Spancill Hill', 'Are ye right there Michael, are ye right?', 'The Lovely Rose of Clare' and 'Lisdoonvarna' by Christy Moore.

Francis Bindon the renowned portrait painter was born in Clare. He was a member of a renowned Ennis family, many of whom represented the Borough of Ennis in the Irish Parliament. The writer and poet, Francis MacNamara was born in Ennistymon.

The scholar, Eugene O'Curry was born in Doonaha in 1794 and became renowned for his outstanding contributions to ordnance survey. The Gaelic writer Micheal O Griofa was also a native of Clare. The Gaelic poet, Brian Merriman was born in Ennistymon in 1747. His most famous work, Cuirt an Mheain Oidhche (The Midnight Court), a bawdy epic of sexual morals that was banned in English but allowed in Irish. The prolific and controversial writer Edna O'Brien was born in Tuamgraney. The song writer and singer, Percy French brought the West Clare Railway to prominence with his 'Are ye Right there Michael, are ye Right?' which was recorded by Brendan O'Dowda.

The sun sets in the West.

In 1990 a major new initiative entitled Rural Resettlement Ireland, was launched in County Clare. The scheme arose out of concern in rural districts by Clare people of the depopulation of their areas with the flight of young people to the cities. This was a voluntary organisation set up to help urban families in congested towns and cities to relocate in the Clare area. A pilot scheme was set up in the Loop Head area and proved a great success. Soon the scheme was extended to other areas of County Clare and later to other counties.

Various areas of County Clare have featured in feature films over the past sixty years. Following the great success of *The Quiet Man* John Ford returned to Ireland in 1956 to film *The Rising of the Moon*. The middle part of the trilogy, *A Minute's Wait*, is based around the Dublin train's halt at a country station and the general chaos that surrounds it and for the sequence a steam train shunted between Kilkee and Moyasta stations. Jimmy O'Dea and Maureen Potter were two of the stars. Much of the location work for *I was Happy Here*, based on the story by Edna O'Brien, was filmed around Lahinch. Sarah Miles and Cyril Cusack starred in the love story. County Clare saw a considerable amount of filming during the summer of 1968 with *Guns in the Heather* and *Alfred the Great* being shot there simultaneously. The former was a Walt Disney production about two boys, played by Kurt Russell and Patrick Dawson who become involved in intrigue and are chased by a gang of crooks. *Alfred the Great* was an epic tale of the bloody battle between the Vikings and Saxons. Replicas of Viking ships sailed up the River Shannon for the battle scenes. David Hemmings played King Alfred and Michael York the Viking. Hundreds of locals grew beards and were recruited as extras. *Joyriders*, a quirky love story of two runaways included scenes that were shot around Kilkee. Director John Huston brought Paul Newman and James Mason to Clare and Galway for *The Mackintosh Man*. This thriller had some spectacular car chases around the Burren. *North Sea Hijack* involved a gang of terrorists who hijacked an oil-rig and held the British Government to ransom for £25 million. Roger Moore and James Mason headed the cast with areas of Clare and Galway doubling for Scotland. Various scenic locations in the county also featured in *Tristan and Isolt* with Richard Burton made in 1979. The film crew for *Hear My Song*, the story of Joseph Locke, also visited Clare particularly around the Cliffs of Moher. Ned Beatty and Shirley Ann Field headed the cast.

West Clare

BALLYVAUGHAN

The attractive village of Ballyvaughan is the most northerly place in County Clare, just inside the County Galway border and in the parish of Drumcreehy. The village, set in a green wooded vale, is a small fishing and trading port on Galway Bay. The name Ballyvaughan in Irish is Baile Ui Bheachain, 'Behan's or Vaughan's Town.'

By the fifth century monks had established monastic settlements in various areas of the Burren and traces of numerous early church ruins in the Ballyvaughan area bear credence to this theory

Ballyvaughan is primarily known for its proximity to the Burren and is an ideal base for exploring this unique landscape. The district has a good selection of hotels, guest-houses, B&Bs and a number of rent-a-cottage schemes. There are restaurants and pubs aplenty. The traveller should explore Black Head with its views over Galway Bay, the Aran Islands and the Cliffs of Moher. The circular road from Ballyvaughan to Blackhead, Ballylacken and Lisdoonvarna and returning by way of the Corkscrew Hill displays a spectacular variety of sea and mountain views. The Black Head lighthouse was erected in 1936.

In 1829 a new quay was built in Ballyvaughan by the Fishery Board to cope with the growth of the fishing industry. Prior to the construction of the pier ships would anchor in Ballyvaughan Bay and transfer their cargoes onto smaller craft that would transfer them ashore. In 1837 a further pier was added as the village grew in size. Turf was imported from Galway and Connemara and local commodities such as wheat, vegetables and livestock were transported by boat. Steamers brought visitors from Galway, forming the basis of a thriving tourist industry. From the mid-nineteenth century there was considerable activity in the community. A coastguard station, police barracks and church were built. Each Thursday there was a market for corn and pigs. Every six weeks a court was held and district courts were held regularly. Over the past half century commercial use of the harbour has declined significantly. The harbour is now primarily used for pleasure craft, a sailing fleet and as a departure point for boat trips to the Aran Islands.

Close to Ballyvaughan there is one of the finest cahers or circular stone forts in the county. The huge structure, over 150 feet in diameter, is known as Ballykinvarragh – Baile Cinn Margaid, 'The Town at the Head of the Market.' Nearby is the old ruined church of Noughavel and graveyard. Beside the church there are the remains of the oratory.

Southwest of Ballyvaughan is Newtown Castle, a sixteenth-century tower house, five storeys high, square at the base and circular at the top. There are guided tours of the restored castle, with exhibits of local and natural history of the Burren and a facsimile copy of the Book of Kells. Tour Trails include archaeological and floristic and from pre-Victorian lime kilns to Bronze Age fulachta fiadh.

Further north at Bell Harbour or Bealachugga (Bellmouth), the traveller should take a sharp turn north and take the N67 road left for New Quay. Following the road west to Finavarra Point there is a Martello Tower in a prime location. The tower was one of many erected by the British along the Clare coast around 1810 when they feared a French invasion of Ireland. The towers were manned by small garrisons that were within easy range of each other to facilitate relaying messages back to headquarters in the event of an invasion. As the threat of invasion diminished the towers were abandoned.

Other important estates in the vicinity in the early nineteenth century included Ballyallaban, Muckinish, Sans Souci and Harbour Hill. In 1837, Samuel Lewis during his visit recorded that there were 1,758 inhabitants within the parish of Drumcreehy and 23 houses in the village of Ballyvaughan.

The workhouse in Ballyvaughan was the main centre for the poor and homeless from the late 1830s. Destitute families from small hamlets across the Burren flocked there in large numbers. A major casualty of the period was the small village of Formoyle that has been deserted since famine times. Remains of the houses can still be seen today.

At New Quay is Mount Vernon Lodge, the summer residence of the Gregorys of Coole Park, where Lady Gregory played host to such illustrious figures as W.B. Yeats, John Millington Synge and George Bernard Shaw. Some of the discussions on the setting up of the Abbey Theatre, in Dublin in 1904 took place at this venue. New Quay featured in Shaw's play, *Back to Methuselah*.

Nearby in Parkmore, there is a pillar monument to the Irish poet, Donnchadh Mor O'Dalaigh. The O'Dalaighs (O'Dalys) were hereditary poets to the Loughlens, Lords of the Burren. Beside Parkmore there are the ruins of a bardic school run and staffed by the O'Dalaighs from the fourteenth to the seventeenth centuries. On the outskirts of the village are the remains of Gragan Castle, a tower house that was erected in the sixteenth century. The site of the present Gregan's Castle Hotel was awarded to George Og Martyn, a Cromwellian officer, for services to the Crown.

Aillwee Cave, Ballyvaughan, c. 1992.

Aillwee Cave, 2 miles south-east of Ballyvaughan, is one of the most popular tourist attractions in the county. The cave, in the Burren National Park, extends 0.8 miles into the heart of the mountain and guides escort visitors into this two million year old cave to view stalagmites, stalactites and a waterfall. In 1944 a herdsman, Jack McGann discovered Aillwee Caves when his dog disappeared into a hole in Aillwee Hill. Jack followed him and discovered the spectacular cave, passages, caverns and underground rivers. In 1976 the McGanns opened the caves as a tourist attraction. The symbol for the Aillwee Caves is a bear, referring to the bones of bears that were discovered there. Subsequent excavations found pug marks indicating that bears had hibernated in the caves. The cave contains some impressive stalactites and stalagmites. There are many more extensive caves throughout the north Burren area. Although many are known, only a few have been explored and are open to the public.

At Corcomroe is the site of a Cistercian priory founded in 1180 by King Donal Mor O'Brien. The first monks came from Inishlounagh in County Tipperary, a Cistercian abbey dating from 1148. The church is well preserved and among the ruins are fragments of a cloister and a gatehouse. The church is reputed to be the burial place of King Conor O'Brien who died in 1267. The building has a primitive effigy of O'Brien. In 1317 Dermot O'Brien rested his troops here the night before the great Battle of Dromhirgan. The battle was fought on the ridge to the west of the abbey, between the rival princes of the royal house of O'Brien. The bodies of the slain were laid out in the abbey. Nearby in

Showing the way, Ballyvaughan, 2004.

The sea-facing cliffs of the Burren.

Turloch Hill there is a small lake. South of Turloch Hill is Slieve Carran, about 1,000 feet high that is worth the climb for the view from the summit.

On the southern shore of Galway Bay is Gleninagh Castle, built in the fifteenth century by the O'Loughlens. Close to the castle there is a holy well that is reputed to have healing properties for eye infections.

THE BURREN

The Burren is a unique, almost lunar-like, region of bare carboniferous limestone covering about a hundred square miles in North Clare, surrounded on each side by Ballyvaughan, Lahinch, Ennis, Corofin and the Cliffs of Moher to the north of Lisdoonvarna. The word Burren in Irish is Boireann, 'Great Rock' or 'Rocky Place,' which graphically describes this district with a number of unusual features. Geologists describe the area as 'Karst' and is similar to a stretch of land in Slovenia. When the porous limestone came into contact with the melting ice flow it resulted in the bare, fissured layers that is still evident today.

Below the surface of the Burren there is the most extensive range of rare plant life in Ireland. In late May and early June the gentians, cranebill, geraniums and orchids blossom. Arctic alpine mountain avens grow over the rocks. Irish saxifrage turf crawls over the boulders. There is a unique combination of north/south plants, Mountain avens, Bloody Cranesbill and Spring Sandwort.

A stone wall in the Burren.

A view through the wall.

A lone tree in the Burren.

The landscape dates from before the Ice Age and has been further weathered by rain, frost and storm. Over the centuries rain water has drained through rocks to create caves and underground rivers and lakes. During spells of heavy rainfall it is common for turloughs, or temporary lakes, to flood the fields and then disappear equally as fast.

The archaeology, caves, history, flora, pot-holes, turloughs and folklore all contribute to make this the most fascinating landscape in the country. The limestone rises in terraced hills to over 1,000 feet. There are still hundreds of stone forts and megalithic tombs scattered across the Burren. It is not difficult to understand why early monks and religious people found this location so inviting for a life of solitude and prayer.

The poet, John Betjeman wrote of the Burren:

> *Stony, seaboard, far and foreign,*
> *Stony hills poured over space,*
> *Stony outcrop of the Burren,*
> *Stones in every fertile place,*
> *Little fields with boulders dotted,*
> *Grey stone shoulders saffron spotted*
> *Stone-walled cabins thatched with reeds*
> *Where a Stone Age people breeds*
> *The last of Europe's Stone Age race.*

Poulnabrone portal tomb.

A stone wall in the Burren.

Some have referred to the Burren as resembling a section of the moon with its greyish white surface. It was this area that caused a Cromwellian officer to make the noted observation that 'there was no tree from which to hang a man, no water in which to drown him and no soil in which to bury him.'

The great Poulnabrone Portal Dolmen (the pool of Sorrows), one of the most impressive features in the Burren, is on the Corofin to Ballyvaughan Road. This megalithic monument is comprised of two slabs sitting lengthwise and resting against the outer sides of the upright portal stones, the entire structure covered by a large capstone. The dolmen would originally have been enclosed within a cairn. In 1986 the Office of Public Works carried out extensive excavations on Poulnabrone tomb. The dig uncovered the remains of over twenty adults and juveniles. Radiocarbon dating of the remains suggested that the burials occurred between 3800 and 3200 BC.

Nearer to Killinaboy, in the upland part of the Burren, close to the village of Carran, is the great stone fort of Cahercommaun. The fort is believed to have been occupied during the eighth and ninth centuries by a community that bred livestock, hunted red deer and grew grain. The promontory-style fort, situated on a cliff edge, is now a national monument. Excavations over the decades have unearthed valuable finds including two souterrains, bone pins and a bell.

Within range of the fort is Glasgeivnagh Hill, where Lon the Smith, a member of the Tuatha De Danann was reputed to have taken refuge. There are many myths and legends told about this infamous character including the fact that he had three hands and made weapons.

Another important feature of this area is Killinaboy church that dates from the seventh century. The original church is believed to have been founded on this site and derives its name from Cill Inghean Bhuidhe, the Church of the Daughter of Boetius. She was a patron of the Dalcassians. In later centuries the church was extended and renovated.

James Plunkett, in *The Gems She Wore,* wrote of the Burren:

Saint Colman built his hermitage in the Burren country on the slopes of Sliabh Corran. There is a story that at the end of Lent, Colman and his servants had no food to break their long, penitential fast. Meanwhile, a feast was taking place at the palace of Colman's half-brother, King Guaire, which was at Kinvara, some miles away. The saint, taking pity on his servant, caused the dishes to be lifted from under the noses of the King's guests and wafted over the hills to the hermitage. The guests not unnaturally wondered what was happening and took horses and followed the dishes. King Guaire was so pleased to find his half-brother that he built a monastery there for him in 610, the present Kilmacduagh.

The building of an interpretative centre in the Burren has been a source of controversy for a number of years. The location chosen for the centre was Mullaghmore Mountain, in the south/east of the Burren at Kilnaboy. The issue was the subject of court cases and protests and was finally abandoned.

LISDOONVARNA

The village of Lisdoonvarna is set 400 feet above sea level in the hilly Burren country of North Clare. The name Lisdoonvarna in Irish is Lios Duin Bhearna, 'Fort of the Gap.' The name derives from an earthen fort near the site of the old Lisdoonvarna castle and was known locally as Fairy Hill. There was no village here until the spa became popular.

On the road from Ballyvaughan to Lisdoonvarna there are a series of elevated views of Galway Bay. The district has many leisurely walks and particularly good is the walk across the Lisdoonvarna Bog at Cnoc na Madre where the variations in the texture of bog and sea and mountain air can be experienced. There is also a recommended two-mile circular walk via the Spectacle Bridge.

The village developed at the beginning of the eighteenth century around a spa based around three mineral springs. The existence of iron, magnesium and sulphur in the water were identified as beneficial for the treatment of various ailments from

Bridge and castle ruin, near Liscannor, 2004.

arthritis to rheumatism and lumbago. A local doctor is credited with having had the water analysed and the results proved the beneficial effects of the water. The waters may also owe something to the natural radioactivity present in them and along with the springs there is a pump room and baths for those who come to take the waters. In 1860 the spa gardens and pump-house were constructed. Local landlords, particularly the Gutherie family, were behind much of the development. The buildings were built to the best contemporary design with tiled floors and marble tables.

In the late 1850s a Protestant church was built in the village. A decade later a simple Catholic church was erected. Prior to this Catholics from the area and visitors attended mass in a 'Mass House' at Toomaghera. During the peak season additional priests had to be drafted in to cope with the large attendances as up to 100 masses per day were celebrated. To cope with the growing numbers of visitors, hotels and guest-houses began to mushroom in the locality. By the late 1870s, Lisdoonvarna had five large hotels – The Hydro, The Imperial, The Thomond, The Royal Spa and The Atlantic View.

From the 1870s the Midlands Great Western Railway advertised holidays in Lisdoonvarna and visitors could travel by steamer from Galway to Ballyvaughan and hence by coach or trap to the spa. The operation became more professional and sulphur was dispensed from a pump-house. A decade later, with the introduction of the West and South Clare Railways and the opening of a station at Ennistymon, passengers were transferred by various forms of transport to Lisdoonvarna. Hotels and guest-houses began to spring up to cater for the large influx of visitors.

Spa house and baths, Lisdoonvarna, c. 1911.

Kincora House, Lisdoonvarna, c. 2004.

The famous Spectacle Bridge is a short distance west of the town where the Aille River flows westwards to Doolin under the Ennistymon Road. The river makes its way through a deep, narrow gorge and the bridge must support the road at one point, 25 metres above the river. The lower arch of the bridge had to be surmounted by another, a double arch forming a circular opening, the combination giving the bridge its distinctive appearance.

Close to Lisdoonvarna is the ruin of the ancient church of Kilmoon and a burial place dating from the fourteenth century. Above the church there is a pillar stone known as The Standing Stone of Kilmoon. Ballynalacken Castle, a fifteenth-century O'Brien stronghold, stands 3 miles north-west of the village. Doolin House was built in Lisdoonvarna in 1639. One of its owners, author and philosopher, Francis MacNamara, entertained such guests as Dylan Thomas and Augustine John at the house. MacNamara's daughter, Nicolette Deva, wrote a book *Two Flamboyant Fathers*, giving an account of his life and times.

In 1840 John O'Brien, High Sheriff of County Clare and Member of Parliament for Limerick, built Ballinalacken House, 2½ miles north-west of the village. His fifth son, 'Peter the Packer', became Lord Chief Justice of Ireland in 1889 and earned his nickname from his habit of 'packing juries,' in order to gain convictions.

The opening of the spa in the nineteenth century was the main reason for the growth and development of the town. In 1859, a Church of Ireland church was built in the village and a number of years later a Catholic church was erected. In 1887, the nearest station opened 7 miles away in Ennistymon but many villagers continued to walk or take a horse and cart. In the late 1930s a new pump-house was erected and in later years there were further modifications with the addition of sulphur baths, a sauna and other specialised treatments.

The only remaining active spa in Ireland, is 2½ miles from Poll na Gollum junction. The spa wells, with their sulphur and chalybeate springs, are still well attended. The waters contain magnesia, iodine and iron and have a high reputation as health restoratives. The Spa Wells Health Centre contains the principal sulphur spring and the centre has a pump-house and baths, including sauna baths, sun lounges, showers and massage rooms and a large recreation hall. The sulphur and chalybeate springs are used principally for rheumatic and glandular ills.

An additional activity associated with Lisdoonvara is matchmaking and the town is undoubtedly the matchmaking capital of Ireland. The custom evolved when bachelor farmers were accustomed, after the harvest was gathered, to go in search of relaxation, take the waters and look for a wife. Traditionally September was the high season in Lisdoonvarna with music and dances in pubs and hotels throughout the day. Dances, ceilis and concerts were held regularly at the Spa Centre too. Still today the practice of morning singsongs and lunchtime dance sessions are characteristic of the 'Ballroom of Romance' tradition. Matchmaker Willie Daly takes groups on 'Romantic Trail Rides' in the hope that romance will blossom!

To the present the Harvest and Matchmaking Festival is held in Lisdoonvarna each September. This ritual has been incorporated into a week of dances and events to encourage single people to find a partner. Old-style dances are held in the hall of the spa gardens and all the pubs and hotels organise special events.

In the 1960s and '70s there were popular folk festivals in Lisdoonvara. These events are encapsulated in the great song *Lisdoonvarna* by Christy Moore.

Three miles north of Lisdoonvarna is Pollynagollum, entrance to one of the longest caves in Ireland. In late spring and early summer the area is a base for those wishing to enjoy the special flora of the Burren at its best.

DOOLIN

Doolin is a small fishing village, on a sandy bay about 2 miles from Aill na Searrach, the northern boundary of the Cliffs of Moher. Doolin was once known as Fisherstreet and was marked so on many early maps. The name Doolin in Irish is Dulainn, 'Black Church.' Another theory of the origin of the name is two pools, Da Linn.

Stone Age man lived in the locality as evidenced by the discovery of axe heads in the sand dunes and there are labyrinthine caves close to the village where he may have lived. A large earthen fort and fosse have been located on a hill overlooking Doolin and at Teergonean there is a cairn.

There is a fishing fleet based at the small harbour and Doolin ferry offers the shortest crossing to Inisheer on the Aran Islands. Today boat trips can also be arranged to view the Cliffs of Moher from the sea. There are also lake shore and deep sea angling facilities in the district. Not far from the pier is an area noted for smuggling and from which the young Irishmen ('Wild Geese') are believed to have set sail in the late seventeenth century to join the French army. Ship's captains gave the young volunteers the name 'Wild Geese' as they were illegal cargoes, signing up to fight against England.

Doolin is one of the best-known villages in County Clare, especially for its strong heritage of traditional music. Since the mid-1950s the village has built up a considerable international reputation due to the achievements of a range of musicians, most notably the Russell brothers, Miko, Gus and Packo. Word of mouth by visiting Germans and Americans drew the crowds to Doolin. Annually the village attracts a continuous stream of music lovers from around the world. Set dancing can also be enjoyed in many venues. The village has gained greatly from the revival of interest in traditional music in recent years that attracts enormous crowds to festivals, or fleadhanna, of Irish and international music and dance. After dark is when the sleepy village of Doolin really comes alive to the lilt of music.

Doolin Ferry anchored in Ballyvaughan, 2004.

There are many remains of castles, forts and churches amongst the surrounding countryside. South of Doolin, on the road to Liscannor is the cylindrical Doonagore castle, a magical structure, consisting of a circular tower in a small bawn or walled enclosure. This is one of the three cylindrical medieval tower houses in North Clare. The other two are at Newtown and Fanore. In the fourteenth century Teigue MacTurlough MacCon O'Connor built Doonagore castle. In 1588, at the time of the Spanish Armada, the High Sheriff of Clare, Boetius MacClancy and a strong force were based at Doonagore castle. From here he despatched troops to apprehend any Spaniards who were washed ashore and put them to death. The bodies of the Spaniards were buried in a mound near the present Roman Catholic Church of the Holy Rosary.

Early in the nineteenth century, Iron Age burial remains were discovered within the environs of the Doonagore castle. This is evidence also that Mesolithic people inhabited this area. The castle remained under the control of the O'Connors for many centuries. Recently the castle was restored and is now a private residence. Close to Fisherstreet there are the remains of another O'Brien castle.

In the early 1900s, Doolin House was host to many literary and artistic figures including George Bernard Shaw, W.B. Yeats, Augustus John and Lady Gregory. While resident in the house, Augustus John painted many landscapes and local characters. One of his best-known paintings is of a woman who served as a watch-out for the poitin makers in the district. In 1920 the IRA destroyed the house.

There are a variety of caves within a small radius of the village. Flagstones from the area have been used in buildings in Dublin and London.

Old farmyard in Doolin.

Doonagore Castle, near Doolin, 2004.

Traditional cottage, Doolin.

Visitors are advised to abandon their cars and take to foot or bicycle to really experience the true beauty of the district.

CLIFFS OF MOHER

The road south from Lisdoonvarna leads to one of the most famous landmarks in the country, the Cliffs of Moher that drop vertically to the Atlantic Ocean. The cliffs climb to 656 feet and stretch almost 5 miles in length, standing defiantly as natural ramparts, of alternating shale and flagstone, against the ferocity of the ocean. The formation of the cliffs can be dated to the Carboniferous period or to the fifth period in the Palaeozoic era. The name of the cliffs in Irish is 'Mionnan Motar, The Rocky Diadem of the Ruined Stone Fort.' The cliffs take their name from an ancient promontory fort, Motair, that once stood on Hag's Head until it was removed in the twentieth century and replaced by a signal tower.

Climbing up from O'Brien Tower is Aillenasharragh, the Cliff of the Foals. Further on is Kilcroney known as the Cave of the Wild Horses. Both of these feature in a legend involving the Tuatha De Danaan when with their magical powers they changed themselves into horses and remained in the caves for many years. Many centuries later, so the legend goes, foals suddenly appeared from these caves and being alarmed at the outside world charged over the cliff to their death.

In 1835 the notorious landlord, Cornelius O'Brien from Birchfield House, erected the O'Brien Tower at the summit as an observation post for visitors. From the vantage point of this gothic tower it is possible to view the Clare coastline, the Mountains of Kerry and Connemara, the Aran Islands and the Twelve Ben's. Hag's Head is located at the southern end of the cliffs.

During the famine years O'Brien gave relief work to his own tenants and angered other members of the community that were also suffering. In the locality it was said that 'he built everything around here except the Cliffs of Moher.' O'Brien, known locally as Corney was a Liberal Member of Parliament for Clare for over twenty years from the 1830s. He supported the repeal of the Act of Union and was chairman of the committee that selected Daniel O'Connell as candidate for Clare. One of his most unusual schemes was the erection of the O'Brien Monument in his own honour, close to Saint Brigid's Well.

Saint Brigid is one of the most popular saints in Ireland and many Irish people are still devoted to her. On her feast day, 15 August each year, crowds still visit the Holy Well to pray, sing hymns and leave petitions in an age-old tradition.

During the nineteenth century, several quarries opened along the cliffs and flagstones were extracted. The flagstones were transferred to Liscannor where they were transported throughout Ireland and shipped to England for building purposes. Flagstones from the district were used in the construction of the Royal Mint in London and the Redemporist church in Belfast.

Cliffs of Moher, c. 1907.

Cliffs of Moher, c. 1990.

In 1972 the writer, James Plunkett recorded the following:

The Cliffs of Moher rise 700 feet above the sea and extend for 5 miles, so sheer and inhospitable that even the sea birds seem to have despaired of finding any shelter for nesting. In misty weather they look even more enormous, like the nightmare of some deranged God; in fine weather, particularly at sunset, they belong still to mythology and the underworld. I remember one magnificent evening of calm sea and barely perceptible wind, when they seemed, for all their dark and massive brutality, to have become weightless in a world of such liquidity and colour that it was impossible to say if the ocean was reflecting the sky or the sky the ocean.

There is a visitor's centre by the cliffs that provides information and includes a craft shop, tea-rooms and a large car park. The view is breathtaking and on a clear day it is possible to enjoy excellent panoramic views of the surrounding countryside. There is a walk of approximately 4 miles along the cliff paths beginning at the car park on the Lisdoonvarna Road. There is another worthwhile walk along a track up the steep hill to the highest point of the cliffs between O'Brien Tower and Aillenasharragh. The cliffs have featured in many films including *The Mackintosh Man* with Paul Newman, in which a Mercedes drove over the edge and *Hear My Song* with Ned Beatty.

KILFENORA

The small market village of Kilfenora is 5 miles south-east of Lisdoonvarna, in a remote part of west Clare, set in a hollow of hills in the centre of the Burren. The name Kilfenora in Irish is Cill Fionnurach, 'The Church of Finnabair.'

In the sixth century, Saint Fachtnan is believed to have founded a church here.

Kilfenora was once of such ecclesiastical importance that it was the Episcopal See of the ancient Kilfenora diocese. In the sixth century its first bishop was Saint Fachtna who founded a church here. The feast day of Saint Fachtna, who also had associations with Rosscarbery in County Cork, is 14 August.

In 1055 Murrough O'Brien, one of the Dal gCais kings attacked Kilfenora Abbey and killed many of the monks. In 1079 it was plundered by the Vikings and was attacked again in 1100. In 1111, when the Synod of Rathbreasail divided Ireland into dioceses and parishes, Kilfenora was overlooked. The building was later rebuilt as a cathedral but is now reduced to the status of a parish church. In 1152 at the Synod of Kells, Kilfenora was declared a diocese, containing the barony of the Burren and Corcumroe. It was the smallest and poorest diocese in the country and in 1172 the Bishop of Kilfenora took the oath of loyalty to King Henry II. Records indicate that the bishop remained unnamed and his successors were known only by their initials. The first named bishop, Johannes, was appointed in 1224 and many of his successors in the thirteenth and fourteenth centuries were only known by their Christian names.

From 1572-1647 Kilfenora had no bishop. Today Kilfenora is administered by the Bishop of Galway and is unique in Ireland as having the Pope as its bishop. The old church, a small building with a square tower now partly roofless, became the Cathedral. Only the nave is now in use, having been incorporated into the Church of Ireland church

There are a number of buildings and sites of importance within the environs of Kilfenora. Six miles east of the village is the ruin of Killinaboy's ancient church and the stump of a round tower. Two miles north-east of Kilfenora is Ballykinvarragh, one of the largest Iron Age stone forts in western Europe. The fort, about fifty metres in diameter, is a large caher, with a circle of stones around it. A mile north-west at Kilcameea, there is a mound believed to be the site of Saint Caimin's church that was built in the seventh century. Another ancient church near Kilfenora is Kilcorney church, of which only the ruins remain today. West of the village there is the ruin of the old church of Kilcarragh that is reputed to have been once a hospital for lepers. To the north there is a holy well.

About 3 miles from the village, on the road to Corofin, is the ruined Lemaneh castle and Manor House that belonged to Donal O'Brien. The castle's tower, dating from 1480, is believed to have been constructed by Turlough Donn, one of the smaller kings of the area. The name Leamaneh refers to Leim an Eich, meaning 'The Horse's Leap.' In 1548 Turlough Donn's son, Murrough was appointed First Earl of Thomond by King Henry VIII. Murrough's son, Donough inherited Leamaneh and his other property but in 1580 he was hanged in Limerick and the property passed to his son, Conor. In 1640, a later descendant, also Conor O'Brien built the adjoining four-storey residence. With the castle at this strategic location he was able to control the immediate roads to the Burren.

Conor's wife was the independently-minded Maire Rua MacMahon, noted for some legendary exploits. During Conor's absence she is reputed to have taken multiple lovers. She was an insanely jealous woman and would treat her attractive female staff in a harsh manner. In 1651 Conor O'Brien and a force set out to stop Cromwell's son-in-law, Henry Ireton attacking from the Limerick direction. O'Brien and many of his force were killed. Maire finding herself a widow and in a vulnerable position married a Parliamentary officer, Captain John Cooper, to prevent her lands being confiscated. Her son, Donough inherited the property and in 1685 he transferred the family residence to Dromoland Castle. No other member of the O'Brien family lived at Leamaneh Castle.

Another important site in the vicinity is the ringfort, on the edge of a ravine, south of Carron. The structure was erected in the ninth century and in 1934 the site was excavated and it is now preserved as a national monument.

One of the most significant people associated with the district is Michael Cusack who was born in a cottage in Carron. He became an all-round sportsman and strongly believed that hurling and Gaelic football should be restored to their national place. On 1 November 1884 at a meeting of the Gaelic Athletic Association (GAA) in Hayes' Hotel, Thurles, he became a founding member of the association.

Another important feature of Kilfenora is its High Crosses. There were so many high crosses in the grounds of Kilfenora cathedral that it became known as 'The City of the Crosses.' There are still six crosses in the area, the seventh was transferred to Killaloe. One of the best-known is the Doorty Cross (O Dughartaigh – a Tipperary family with heredity rights to the bishopric), standing to the west of the cathedral. One face of the cross illustrates Kilfenora's change from monastic status, dating from around 1152. There is also 'The Cross in the Field' at the west door, another High Cross and several smaller crosses in the graveyard.

In 1820, when Bishop Richard Mant visited Kilfenora, he gave the following account: 'it is the worst village that I have seen in Ireland, and in the most desolate and least interesting country.' In 1825 the Catholic bishop of Kilmacduagh and Kilfenora, Dr Edmund French, built nine new churches in the parish to cope with the growing population. The majority of the population was Catholic as is shown in a census of 1868 when the population of the diocese was recorded as 23,042 with only 224 members of the Church of Ireland.

A date that is still remembered in the district is April 1862 when there was an outbreak of fever that resulted in many deaths among the poor who were living in deplorable conditions.

In 1981 Reverent Walton Empey was appointed as the Church of Ireland bishop of Kilfenora.

The picturesque road to Kilfenora runs along the south-west boundary of the Burren through state forests. The Burren Display Centre (Bru na Boirne), located in Kilfenora, was established by a local co-operative body to develop the area as a centre for touring and information on the Burren. There are displays of butterflies, flora, fauna and rock formations that can be found in the district. The audio-visual and guides reveal facts on the history that has shaped the Burren as one of the most intriguing natural attractions in Europe. This was one of the first Interpretative Centres in Europe.

Kilfenora is also a lively spot for traditional music, ceili dancing and set-dancing weekends. The Kilfenora Ceili Band, one of the most popular ceili bands in Ireland, was established in the village early in the twentieth century and began a tradition that has been maintained at a high level ever since. They are the All-Ireland Ceili band champions and have made many tours to the United States and England. During the summer months, painting classes by leading artists are held in the village

In recent years Kilfenora has become familiar to a world-wide audience as the main location for the award-winning television series *Father Ted*. The series written by Graham Lenihan and Arthur Matthews was filmed on location around Kilfenora, Ennistymon and Kilnaboy. The *Father Ted* stories told of the misadventures of three off-the-wall priests on Craggy Island and starred Dermot Morgan, Ardal O'Hanlon, Frank Kelly, and Pauline McLynn as their house-keeper.

LISCANNOR

Liscannor is a small picturesque fishing village on the R478 road, at the northern end of Liscannor Bay, midway between Lahinch and the Cliffs of Moher. The name Liscannor in Irish is Lios Ceannuir, 'Ceannur's Fort.' A small harbour was built on the site of an old fort of that name. In around AD 800 an enormous wave is reputed to have hit Mutton Island, off Liscannor Bay, and split it.

Liscannor is an unusual village as virtually all its inhabitants live on one side of the street. The village is noted for its Fossilite Flag-Stones.

On the northern shore of Liscannor Bay is the medieval church of Kilmacreehy, Cill Mac Creithe na Tragha. The original church, also known as Saint Macreehy's church, with a nave and chancel was erected in the early twelfth century, on the site of a school founded by Saint Macreehy. Close to the church and graveyard is a holy well that is reputed to have healing powers for disorders of the eyes and other diseases. In the graveyard there is the unmarked grave of the great eighteenth century scholar, Hugh MacCurtin.

In the mid-sixteenth century Theo O'Connor built Liscannor Castle on the point. In 1582 the castle, in a prime defensive position, was granted to Sir Donal O'Brien and

Liscannor castle, c. 2004.

became his stronghold. In 1588, at the time of the Spanish Armada and a threatened Spanish invasion of Ireland, Turlough O'Brien occupied the castle.

In 1770 it was recorded that in Liscannor there were small cabins along the original 'street' that ran parallel with the coastline. The bridge, close to the village, was built in 1845 and is still known as 'the new bridge.'

It has been long believed that the submerged reef in Liscannor Bay indicates the location of the 'lost city' of Cill Stuitin, 'the Church of Kilstephen.' According to legend, the key of the church is said to be buried with the Ossianic hero, Conan, under his pillar stone on Slieve Callan and an ancient village and church once stood there; now only the reef of Kilstuithin remains.

John Philip Holland, the inventor of the submarine, was born in Castle Street (renamed Holland Street in his honour) in Liscannor on 24 February 1841. He was

Liscannor harbour, c. 1990.

educated by the Christian Brothers in Ennistymon and Limerick. As a boy in the village, Holland was interested in the sea and from an early age he began to design submarines and the Fenians became interested in his invention as a potential weapon against British boats. However, Holland emigrated to Boston and his Holland VI submarine was commissioned by the United States Navy in 1900. The submarine employed electric motors under water and a gasoline engine on the surface. Thereafter submarines were to play a vital part in warfare particularly from 1914 in The First World War. Holland died in 1914 and in 1977 the United States Navy presented a headstone commemorating his career to the people of Liscannor. The headstone is now in the local community centre by the harbour.

About 2 miles north-west of Liscannor, on the road to the Cliffs of Moher, there is a high pillar known as the O'Brien Monument. In 1853 Cornelius O'Brien MP and owner of Birchfield House, erected it at the expense of his reluctant tenants. He chose the wording of the inscription that highlighted his virtues. The monument anticipated his death by three years.

Close by is the Holy Well of Saint Brigid, the waters of which are believed to have curing properties. O'Brien erected the monument in its present location in thanksgiving for a cure of an ailment. Pilgrims travel to the well from all over County Clare and the Aran Islands on the last Sunday in July for the Lughnasa festivities. The longstanding tradition of the blessing of the boats also occurs on this day. Celebrations for Lughnasa continue into the following Sunday when they are transferred to Lahinch.

Lahinch

The town of Lahinch is situated at the head of Liscannor Bay beside a long beach of golden sand. The town was previously known as Leath Inse or peninsula, from its position on the southern shore of the bay. The old Irish word for Lahinch was Leacht Ui Chocchuir, 'The Tomb of O'Connor' – the chieftain of an old local Celtic clan, who is reputed to have been buried there.

According to legend the sand dunes are said to have been the haunt of Dona, the Fairy King. North of Lahinch at O'Brien Bridge, there are the remains of Dough Castle built by Donnchadh O'Connor in 1442. Later the O'Brien clan occupied the castle.

Lahinch began to develop gradually from the middle of the eighteenth century. In 1887 the town came to prominence as a holiday resort when it was connected to the West Clare Railway and people could travel there from Limerick, Ennis and the adjoining counties. The songwriter, Percy French, wrote 'at Lahinch the sea shines like a jewel.'

In 1893 an impressive promenade was built parallel to the sea, to cater for the growing numbers of visitors to the resort. Soon it became one of the most popular holiday destinations on the west coast. In the original town most of the buildings were along the sea front, with only two inland streets. Lahinch beach has a long crescent-shaped shoreline that faces out into the open Atlantic Ocean and has a wide mouth.

Lahinch seafront, c. 1995.

The shape of the resort creates Atlantic breakers that attract surfing and canoeing enthusiasts from all over the world. Other water sports including sailing, swimming, skin-diving, deep-sea and fresh-water fishing can be enjoyed in the locality.

Lahinch is regarded as a premier resort for golfers and can boast of two eighteen-hole golf courses – Lahinch Golf Course and Castle Golf Course. In 1892 the officers of the Scottish Black Watch, who were stationed in Limerick, established the Lahinch Championship course. One event not easily forgotten in Lahinch took place in September 1920. Following an ambush in Rineen in which the IRA killed six RIC men, the Black and Tans ransacked Lahinch and three local men were shot dead. Another young man was burned alive in his house and a forth man died some days later from his wounds. A daring golfer raised the tricolour at the golf club but the British pulled it down and burned it.

During the summer months the resort comes alive with music and dance, catering for all ages. Close to the promenade there is an entertainment centre with a swimming pool, playrooms and tennis court and a new amenity is the Seaworld Leisure Centre.

Bird watchers enjoy exploring the marshes north of the town that houses a wide variety of terrestrial, freshwater and marine birds.

ENNISTYMON

The town of Ennistymon is picturesquely situated on the River Cullenagh (or Ennistymon River), where it passes over the falls. The river rises in the mountains to the south-east and meanders through Ennistymon, a small market town, neatly laid out along a central street that runs to Saint Andrews Church of Ireland church. The town can be reached from Ennis on the N85 road through Inagh. The name Ennistymon in Irish is Inis Diomain, 'Diaman's River Crossing.' In 580 Saint Mainchin built a church on a hill overlooking the river. The remains of this church are in the graveyard of the Catholic parish church.

Ennistymon is 2½ miles inland from Lahinch, in a wooded valley. The Falls Hotel is situated on a high elevation above the river, an area that was once an island. The hotel once known as the Ennistymon Hotel was built in 1764, on the site of an O'Brien castle.

There are many attractive traditional shop fronts in the main street that receive favourable comments from visitors and travel writers and the village offers a good selection of accommodation, pubs and restaurants.

In 1422 the Annals of the Four Masters recorded: 'A moated O'Connor castle at Inisdyman.' In 1588 Turlough O'Brien erected a tower house in the area. Lord Clare, of the chief Clare family, the O'Briens, was loyal to James II and was awarded 57,000 acres in the district. At the beginning of the eighteenth century enormous tracts of land were divided amongst newcomers. Up to the middle of the century, the area around Ennistymon was beyond the British authorities as the roads were almost impassable.

Off to the creamery, Ennistymon, c. 1988.

A happy man in Ennistymon, 2004.

Traditional shop front in Ennistymon, 2004.

In 1770 the town began to grow up around the shallow crossing of the river. Twenty years later the fine stone bridge of seven arches was constructed and it became one of the main factors in the development of the town.

In 1778 Revd James Kenny, a Protestant clergyman, who had converted from Catholicism built the old church of Ennistymon on the site of Saint Mainchin's church overlooking the town. In 1824 the Christian Brothers opened a school in Ennistymon in the old church building. Six years later the Church of Ireland church was no longer used for public worship and the new Church of Saint Andrew was built by a grant of £1,000 from the Board of First Fruits and Tenths. The old church building was renovated and used as an Irish Music and Dance Centre.

In 1837 Samuel Lewis visited the town and gave the following account in *Lewis's Topographical Dictionary*:

> Ennistymon, a market and post-town containing 241 houses and 1,430 inhabitants. The town, though irregularly built, has a picturesque appearance. This place had formerly a considerable market for strong knit woollen stockings. The Market, which is held on Saturday, is well supplied with provisions, and is also a good market for corn and pigs. Adjoining the town is Ennistymon Castle, formerly a seat of the O'Brien family, and now the residence of Andrew Finnucane, Esq. At a short distance is the glebe-house, the residence of Archdeacon Whitty.

Eugene's, Ennistymon, 2004.

This area suffered badly in the famine period where many of the peasants lived in humble dwellings. In September 1845 a workhouse was erected in the town at a cost of £6,600 to house 600 paupers. During the worst period of the famine it was filled to capacity.

In 1881 a travel guide gave the following description of the town: 'The town of Ennistymon, with its first range of shops, large, hotel and good broad streets, is evidently inhabited by men of taste, energy and enterprise.'

The village of Kilshanny, 3 miles north of Ennistymon, has an outdoor Caving Centre. The old Kilshanny church on the east of the main road was an Augustinian Foundation dating to the twelfth century and its original bell of Saint Cuanna is now in the British Museum. There is also a cairn known as Carn Connachtach, eight

Daly's bar, Ennistymon, 2004.

A traditional barber's shop, Ennistymon, 2004.

Ennistymon, 2004.

metres high and about one hundred metres in diameter. According to legend this cairn was known as Carn MacTail as it was the burial place of MacTail, son of Broc, chieftain of Corcomroe and descendants of Corcomroe are believed to have been buried there. Slain members of the Connaught Regiment are also buried there. The most common belief is that the monument is a Bronze Age burial mound. Two miles from Ennistymon is the graveyard of Killaspunghan church and a mound, indicating where an ancient church once stood.

One of the best-known poets in the Irish language, Brian Merriman, was born in 1749 in Ennistymon, the son of a stonemason. He became a teacher and moved to Feakle where he taught from 1765-1785. His most important work, Cuirt an Mhean-Oiche' (The Midnight Court), was written around 1780 and is still unique in Irish literature. It is a long poem in the Bardic tradition when Ireland was in sharp decline and twin forces of clericalism and paternalism were ushering in a new constricting order. While centred on women and their vanishing freedoms, the scope of the poem is much wider. This frolicking, rollicking, bawdy poem was one last great shout of defiance and satire from the old Ireland, in defence of traditional freedoms. Merriman is buried in Feakle graveyard, close to the grave of Biddy Early. An annual summer school is held in the vicinity to commemorate the work of Merriman.

Another native of Ennistymon was the writer and poet, Francis MacNamara who was born there in 1884. He published several books of poetry and edited and translated many volumes of prose. For a period MacNamara was owner of the Falls Hotel that incorporated into its old walls an earlier fortified building. His daughter Caitlin married the Welsh poet, Dylan Thomas, who visited the family there.

On 23 September 1920 Captain Lendrum, Registered Magistrate for Kilkee, was travelling by car to Ennistymon to preside at the petty sessions when the IRA kidnapped him. Eight days later his body was found. As a reprisal the Black and Tans attacked and ransacked Kilrush, Kilkee, Doonbeg, Cooraclare, Mullagh and Quilty, in an attempt to flush out the IRA and their sympathisers.

One interesting grave in the cemetery adjoining the Catholic church is of Edith Eileen Cruise, who died in 1962. She was aunt of Caitlin Thomas, wife of the Welsh poet, Dylan Thomas.

MILTOWN MALBAY

Miltown Malbay, a small market town and holiday resort is located approximately two miles east of Spanish Point. The name Miltown Malbay in Irish is Straid na Cathrach 'Village of the Stone Fort.' Another source gives the translation as Straid na Catrac 'The Street of the Castle.' The town, noted for its limestone flags, is the principal market of West Clare.

Experts differ about the origins of the town's name. Some believe that it devolved from McMahon's corn and woollen mills in the nineteenth century. Other sources believe that, despite the fact that the town lies inland it takes its name from nearby Mal Bay. According to legend, Mal, a witch, pursued Cuchulann to Loop Head. When she attempted to make a long jump like Cuchulann, she fell into the sea and was washed ashore at Mal Bay.

Like so many other areas of County Clare, Miltown Malbay has a rich heritage of traditional music and dance. Every July the Willie Clancy Summer School, dedicated to the memory of Clare's legendary greatest piper, is held there. This leading cultural event was initiated in 1973 and attracts over 7,000 visitors annually to attend the diverse events ranging from workshops of musical instruments and set-dancing. Another major festival is the Merriman Summer School that combines lectures, walks and traditional sessions.

Willie Clancy was born here in 1918, into a musical family. His father, Gilbert, also a gifted musician learned much from the legacy of the blind piper, Garret Barry. Willie began playing the tin whistle at the age of five.

North-west of Miltown Malbay there is the ruin of the fifteenth-century Kilfarboy church. Two outstanding Claremen, Arthur MacCurtain (died 1749), hereditary bard of the O'Briens, and Michael Comyn (died 1760), a distinguished poet and scholar, are buried in the graveyard. There is also a holy well dedicated to Saint Joseph. South westwards from Miltown Malbay the road leads to the Hands Crosswards. Nearby is Slieve Callan, the highest point in West Clare. En route there is a small lake at

Main Street, Miltown Malbay, c. 1890.

Bollynagreana. For centuries the terrain has been known as Cluain Buaile 'Meadow of the Booloying.' On Slieve Callan there is an interesting chamber tomb. Above the lake there is an ogham stone that has been described as a memorial to Conan, a hero of the Fianna but it was later found to be a forgery, erected in the eighteenth century.

The town of Miltown Malbay is a good example of a Victorian resort laid out to a regulated plan, with minor streets branching off the main street. Like other towns the arrival of the railway increased progress with additional houses and shops being erected. The centre of the town developed around the old fort and at Canada Cross at the junction of the Callan and Inagh roads.

From the 1840s Mrs Burdett Moroney, a landlord, was unsympathetic to her tenants and charged high rents and evicted them for non-payment even during the famine. In 1888 the matter came to a head as agitated tenants, supported by the Land League, boycotted Mrs Moroney and her servants. Additional RIC men and troops were drafted in to maintain order. The situation also developed into a boycott of the police and many people were charged and imprisoned. This distrust of the police continued for a considerable time.

On 26 January 1885 Charles Stewart Parnell turned the first sod of the West Clare Railway at Miltown Malbay, that became the terminus of the West Clare Railway and the beginning of the South Clare Railway.

On 14 April 1920 many Republican hunger strikers were released from Mountjoy jail. In Miltown Malbay crowds gathered at Canada Cross to celebrate the event and lit a bonfire and sang and danced. At midnight the RIC arrived and ordered the crowd to disperse. Immediately the police opened fire before the crowd could react. Three people were shot dead and eleven others were wounded. Two days later, at the funeral in Ballard cemetery, hundreds of IRA men attended while the RIC and troops were confined to barracks.

On 22 September 1920, a group from the Fourth Battalion of the IRA, under Captain Ignatius O'Neill, from the cover of a hill at Rineen, north of Miltown Malbay, attacked an RIC patrol travelling from the town to Ennistymon. In the exchange, six policemen were shot dead. Despite the arrival of Black and Tans and British troop reinforcements there were no casualties on the IRA side and they took refuge in the hills. Following the ambush at Rineen the RIC invaded the town, burning buildings and smashing windows. Later that night the Black and Tans joined the RIC and they continued shooting and burning all night. North of Miltown Malbay there is a stone plaque commemorating the ambush.

Also in 1920, Michael Davitt, a Volunteer from Clouna, was shot dead, near Mount Callan, while ambushing an RIC patrol. His colleagues hid his body in the bog. Later that year the Mid-Clare Flying Column ambushed a military convey on 18 December inflicting casualties. Towards the end of the War of Independence, as the Black and Tans were being withdrawn, children jeered them and the Tans opened fire, wounding a number of them.

The former President of Ireland, Patrick J. Hillery, was born in Miltown Malbay on 2 May 1923 to Dr Michael J. Hillery and Ellen McMahon. He was educated at Miltown Malbay National School, Rockwell College and University College, Dublin. He became a medical doctor and was Fianna Fáil TD for Clare from 1951 to 1973. He was Minister for Education (1959-65) and Minister for Foreign Affairs (1962-72). From 1973 to 1976 he was Vice President of the Commission of the European Communities with special responsibility for Social Affairs. He was President of Ireland from 1976 to 1990. Wellington Lodge is an early nineteenth-century house that faced the old race course. The former President's father bought the house and Dr Hillery lived there for a period.

SPANISH POINT

Spanish Point, two miles west of Miltown Malbay, is a small resort, mid-way along the West Clare coast. The Silver Strand at Freagh, two miles north of the village, has been a renowned bathing place for centuries. The name Spanish Point in Irish is Rinn na Spainnear, 'Point of the Spaniards', deriving from the occasion when a large number of Spanish sailors perished there in September 1588 as six ships of the Armada came to grief on the treacherous rocks.

From as far back as the 1820s Spanish Point was a favourite tourist centre where the Moroney family built the Atlantic Hotel, once reputed to be the biggest hotel in the British Isles. The area was frequented by the Victorian middle classes that travelled there from the inland towns and villages of the county. In 1903, during a storm, the Atlantic Hotel, situated on the edge of cliffs, collapsed into the sea. Beneath the cliffs there were stone boxes that filled with seawater with the incoming tide and as the tide went out retained the water so that visitors could immerse themselves in it. At the time it was widely held to have curing properties.

Off the coast of Spanish Point is Mal Bay that is believed to have derived its name from the Latin word Malus meaning evil, from its rugged, dangerous coastline. According to local folklore, the name derives from the red-haired witch, Mal, who, while pursuing Cuchulann at Loop Head, missed a leap onto a rock and fell into the sea. She was washed ashore at Spanish Point, hence the name Mal Bay.

On 15 September 1588 a Spanish Armada ship the *San Marcos* of Portugal, under the captaincy of Marquis of Penafiel, was wrecked on the reef between Mutton Island and Kurgo Point, near Spanish Point. The vessel had a crew of 490 and 33 guns. Some of the drowned crew were buried at Kilfarboy. In all six ships of the Armada came to grief on the treacherous rocks off the West Clare coast. More than 1,000 men were lost and many of their bodies were carried by the tide to Spanish Point. The sailors who swam ashore were butchered by the locals on the orders of the Governor of Connaught, Sir Turlough O'Brien of Liscannor Castle and Boethius Clancy, High Sheriff of Clare and others of high rank. The order handed down was that all the officers and men who survived the shipwreck, were to be immediately put to death. On 20 September 1588 two large Spanish ships were wrecked off the coast with the loss of 700 and the remaining 170 taken prisoner. The survivors were hanged and buried in unmarked graves.

On 18 March 1816, a ship, the *Melanltho*, bound from Limerick to Barcelona, was wrecked off Spanish Point. The crew of seventeen were lost. During the First World War, a ship named the *Kelp* was wrecked in Mal Bay with a cargo of hides and tallow.

QUILTY

Quilty is a small fishing village, south of Spanish Point, on a flat section of the West Clare coast. The name Quilty is an unusual one for an Irish village and derives from the Irish Coillte 'Woods' but there are no woods or forests on this stretch of coastline. It is believed that thousands of years ago before the area was inhabited there was a wood where the village now stands. The remains of tree trunks have been found in the area.

With its close proximity to the Atlantic Ocean it is not surprising that the inhabitants derived most of their livelihood from the sea. There was a long-standing custom of collecting seaweed and spreading it over the stone walls to dry for kelp making. The seaweed was burnt and the ash used to produce iodine or exported for the production of alginates.

Quilty today takes advantage of its closeness to the sea and boats can be hired in the village for deep-sea fishing. For swimmers there are a number of good beaches within easy range of the village.

Mutton Island, about 2 miles off shore, has an interesting history. In 779, according to the Annals of the Four Masters, the island was struck by a tidal wave, causing severe damage. In 1588 some survivors of the Spanish Armada scrambled ashore on Mutton Island. In the early 1800s The British feared that there might be a French invasion on the west coast of Ireland. As a precaution one of a series of signal towers was erected on the island. These towers were erected along the Clare coastline as watch towers to give an alert in the event of an invasion. The invasion never materialised but the towers were later utilised by the coastguard on the lookout for smugglers.

From 1885 with the introduction of the West Clare Railway through the village there was a marked increase in visitors. On 2 October 1907 a French ship named *Leon XIII* of Nantes, with a cargo of wheat, ran aground in a storm off Quilty. Fishermen from the village set out in their currachs to rescue the crew. The majority of the crew was rescued and there was little loss of life. The local curate took advantage of the favourable publicity to launch a fund-raising appeal to build a church. There was an overwhelming response and donations were received locally, nationally and from the United States and England. The French authorities made a small payment to the project. The church, named The Star of the Sea, modelled on an early Christian church, was opened to 1910.

In 1921 Mutton Island was used as a detention centre for offenders under the Sein Féin Courts.

DOONBEG

Doonbeg, known as 'the Long Village' is at the mouth of the Cooraclare or Doonbeg River, on the N67 road from Ennis to Kilkee. Doonbeg in Irish is 'The Small Fort.' To the west of the village there is the townland of Doonmare, in Irish An Dun Mor, 'the Big Fort', which refers to a tower house.

To the north of the village there is a long white strand, framed by sand-dunes. Further north there are the beaches of Seafield and Lough Donnell. An interesting feature of the village is the Doonbeg Development Association Tourist Office. The friendly staff of this centre provide visitors with information for their holidays and can recommend suitable accommodation.

A dominant feature of the village is the remains of the fifteenth-century tower house, standing by the bridge over the Doonbeg River, shortly before it enters the sea. The castle was the fortress of the MacMahons (a descendant of Mahon O'Brien and direct descendant of Brian Boru), and later of the O'Briens. The castle changed owners several times towards the end of the sixteenth century. In 1599 the Earl of

Thomond attacked it and hanged the whole garrison, after they had surrendered. Further along the coast is Killard church, which at various stages has served as both a Catholic and Protestant church. In 1651 it was attacked by Cromwellian troops and badly damaged.

On 29 September 1588 the Spanish Armada ship, *San Estaban* of San Sebastian, part of the squadron of Guipuzeoa, was wrecked in a storm off Doonbeg. The vessel had a crew of 274 men and 26 guns. The vessel ran aground on Doughmore Strand. Some of the crew drowned, the locals killed some more and the remainder were captured by a force under Boetius MacClancy and then executed.

KILKEE

Kilkee is one of the leading seaside resorts in south-west Clare. The town is situated on the N67 road, around a semi-circular bay protected on both sides by low cliffs and a reef called the Duggerna Rocks. With the spring and autumn tides the resort receives the full force of the Atlantic Ocean. The name Kilkee in Irish is Cill Chaoidhe, 'Church of Saint Caoidhe.'

The beach of this popular family resort provides safe natural swimming pools, rock pools and several coves. The Duggerna Rocks, serving as a reef, is a craggy amphitheatre suitable for open-air concerts. One cliff walk stretches 2½ miles from the west end

Kilkee, c. 1954.

A chat on a summer's day, Kilkee, c. 1998.

beginning at Edmund's Point and proceeding to Duggerna Rocks. There is also Pink Cave and Lion Rock and farther along the Puffing Hole. Also within easy reach are Intrinsic Bay, Diamond Rocks and Lookout Hill (200 feet above sea level). From the summit on a clear day it is possible to see the Aran Islands, Twelve Bens, the River Shannon and the Kerry Mountains. The traveller can continue past Bishop's Island, with the ruin of Saint Senan's Oratory. Inland, Fooagh Chalybeate spa, was once a popular place to visit. Further on is the Mermaid's Tunnel, the Sailor's Grave and Castle Point with excellent views along the coast to Loop Head. Another enjoyable walk extends about 5 miles along the east end by Blackrock, the Elephant's Teeth, Burn's Cave, George's Head, Chimney Bay and Hill, into Farrihy Bay and Corbally village.

Kilkee began to develop as a tourist resort in Victorian times when the gentry and professional classes from Ennis and Limerick city built themselves villas. The villas afforded them and their families a break from city life during the summer months with swimming, leisurely strolls and to take the waters of the spa at Footagh. Servants would also accompany the wealthy families. According to the 1831 census the village had a population of 1,051 living in 153 houses. The summer months became known as the 'Kilkee Season' and referred to the tradition of steam vessels bringing visitors from Limerick to Kilrush. Victorian morals were very much in vogue at the time and there were separate bathing boxes for men and women. The wooden bathing boxes were on wheels and could be wheeled to the water's edge protecting the females from unwanted gazes. The men had their own swimming area. The gentry would take

Kilkee Beach, c. 1985.

leisurely strolls along the seafront carrying parasols to protect them from the sun. At this period Kilkee was also known as Doogh, referring to a sandbank.

In November 1850, Edmuns, a three-master emigrant ship bound from Carrigaholt, County Cork to New York was struck by a storm and driven onto Duggerna Rocks in Kilkee Bay. Many of the passengers managed to escape over the rocks but ninety-six people were drowned. Jonas Studdert of Atlantic Lodge, helped in the rescue. The thriller writer, Peter Cheyney, is believed to have been born in Atlantic Lodge in 1896. In 1936 he wrote his first thriller, *This Man is Dangerous* and went onto international success.

The opening of the West Clare Railway in 1885 was to bring a constant flow of day-trippers to the sandy beaches of the area and in 1901 Kilkee became a municipal town. The heydays of Kilkee were from the mid-1850s to the mid-1960s when families returned for annual holidays. The resort was a favourite location with older Anglo-Irish people and the clergy. Entertainment was provided in many of the hotels and during the showband era hundreds of young people were attracted here from the towns of west Clare to dance to their favourite bands.

Unfortunately, from the late 1960s, Kilkee was to suffer the same fate as many other Irish coastal resorts. It was to change from being a fashionable resort to a miniature Blackpool with boarding houses, ice cream parlours, amusement arcades one-armed bandits and singing pubs. There was a shift from traditional holidays with many people opting for package holidays and guaranteed sun and there was a dramatic fall in numbers of visitors.

The two-storey Kilkee station is one of the most impressive buildings in the vicinity. In May 1956 the station was chosen by director John Ford, as one of the main locations for the film, *A Minute's Wait*, from the trilogy, *The Rising of the Moon*. The film starred a host of Irish character actors, headed by Jimmy O'Dea and Maureen Potter. An old steam engine with locomotive No. 5C *The Silver Callan*, shunted carriages between Kilkee and Moyasta, for the filming. In 1969 the distinguished film director, David Lean, moved his production of *Ryan's Daughter*, starring Robert Mitchum, Sarah Miles and John Mills, from the Dingle Peninsula to Kilkee to shoot the film's spectacular storm sequences. Many of the actors and extras put their lives at risk as they off loaded arms on the shore in ferocious conditions. Another film to use Kilkee as a location was *Joyriders* directed by Aisling Walsh in 1968. The scenes for this quirky love story were shot during the off season at the resort.

Kilkee Heritage Centre is a small venue with a collection of exhibitions of household implements and tools and providing an impression of the area's seafaring traditions. There are also old maps and photographs showing the history of the district. The Sweeney Memorial Library, built with the aid of emigrants, is an impressive building and houses an excellent collection of books. The Creegh and Cooraclare rivers, offer good salmon and trout fishing and the scenic drive between Kilkee and the Loop Head peninsula is one of the most spectacular in the country.

Kilrush

The town of Kilrush, the chief market centre of south-west Clare and the second largest town in the county, is situated at the junction of the N68 and N67 roads. Kilrush is a small port and a busy manufacturing town on the northern shore of the Shannon estuary. It was the second largest town in Clare until Shannon was developed from the late 1940s. The name Kilrush in Irish is Cill Ruis, 'the Church of the Promontory' or 'Peninsula Church'. The 'church' refers to an early oratory called Kilkeevan, the church of Kavin, who is reputed to have been a brother of Saint Kevin of Glendalough, County Wicklow.

One mile south of the town there is a good harbour at Cappa or Cappagh Pier (formerly known as Revenue Quay), a good berthing place for vessels that ply between Kilrush and Limerick. In the nineteenth century schooners and steamships travelled from Limerick via Tarbert to Kilrush. From the pier the coastal road extends south-east by the waters edge with good views of Scattery Island and the Shannon Estuary.

In the famous Clare election of 1828 in which Daniel O'Connell stood against the sitting MP for Clare, Vesey Fitzgerald, feelings ran high at the polling booths. The clergy canvassed their congregations and encouraged them to vote en masse for O'Connell. This was very much the case in Kilrush and a newspaper gave the following account:

Between 300 and 400 of John Ormsby Vandeleur's free-holders are now passing up the street to the Court house, preceded by colours, every man with a green leaf in his hand, and amidst the loudest cheering from the towns people. They are western men from Kilrush, and brought in by their clergy to vote for O'Connell. Along the road the general cry of these men was – 'Here's Kilrush, high for O'Connell, high for our priest.' Mr O'Leary the priest of Kilrush, came with them and the town is full of catholic clergy. There are fifteen booths opened for the polling.

Early in the nineteenth century, the Vandeleur family made a generous contribution to the town by building the market square. Colonel John Vandeleur was a notorious landlord noted for high rents and evictions yet several streets in the town are named after members of his family. The main street was improved and several smaller streets were constructed leading off it. By then the town was prosperous as it served as a seaport, market and post town and leading tourist resort. Weekly markets attracted merchants and traders from the surrounding countryside. At that time the British army garrison was based in a three-storey tower in the town centre. In 1848, following the famine, thirty cabins were being demolished daily by the Vandeleurs after their tenants had been evicted for non-payment of rent. This was as a result of the Quarter Acre Clause that denied relief to anyone in possession of more than a quarter acre of land.

The Market house, Kilrush.

On 13 December 1849 a dreadful tragedy befell the area when the ferry returning from Kilrush disintegrated at Poulnasherry Bay with the loss of thirty-four lives. The dead were all paupers from the Loop Head district who had travelled to the workhouse in Kilrush seeking work on relief schemes. The bodies of men, women and children were washed up on the seashore. In a storm on the night of 18 November 1850, the ferryboat from Kilrush to Tarbert sank and nineteen cattle jobbers on board were drowned.

At the height of the famine there were more people living in the Kilrush area than in Ennis. This was mainly due to the fact that there were more famine relief schemes in operation and able bodied men travelled there to seek employment. Inmates of the workhouse also added to the large increase in the population.

On 13 August 1892 the first section of the Kilrush to Kilkee railway line opened with three trains running in each direction daily. The town was provided with a large station with an attractive veranda overhanging the building. The West Clare Railway line was closed on 31 January 1961.

By the late 1800s Kilrush had become a busy trading centre with steamers from Limerick bringing timber and farm produce and transporting material manufactured in the town. The steamers also connected with the West Clare Railway to bring passengers to Kilkee.

W.P. (Percy) French, the famous Irish songwriter, poet, painter and entertainer, whose ballad, 'Are ye Right there Michael, Are ye Right?', is the epitome of the West Clare railway and will ensure its memory lives on forever. The song was written in a house in Kilrush, while he was staying with a friend called Glynn, after his disastrous journey, unaware that Glynn's family were shareholders in the railway. 'Michael' was Michael Talty, for many years head porter at Kilrush but was a guard on French's train. The song was based on an incident on 10 August 1896 when French was en route by train to Kilkee for a concert. The train broke down and there was a delay of three hours as 350 people waited in Moore's Concert Hall for French.

In 1935 members of the Old IRA formed the West Clare Ceili Band in Kilrush in order to revive traditional music and dancing in the locality. The formation of the band generated around a live radio broadcast in February 1936 and thereafter they continued to play at local ceilis and in the famous Mrs Crotty's pub in Kilrush.

The fine harbour has been developed into one of the first west coast marinas and has berthage for 250 boats. The Kilrush Creek Marina, opened in 1991, is fully equipped and accessible at all times. A Marina Centre Village Holiday accommodation and other marina related industries are all located in the development.

There are good recreational facilities in the area including a tennis court, equestrian centre and golf course. Kilrush Woods, east of the town, is an amenity area with woodland walks. In the square there is the Maid of Erin memorial that commemorates the Manchester Martyrs who were executed in 1867. In the Catholic church there are some fine Harry Clarke stained glass windows.

A long-standing tradition in Kilrush has been the Blessing of the Boats. For over two centuries the boats have gathered on the seashore for the blessing. Fishermen and their families line up with pleasure craft owners as the priest reads from Saint Matthew's Gospel about Jesus and his disciples on a boat in a storm.

In the town hall there is an exhibition and audio-visual interpretation entitled 'Kilrush in the Landlord Times,' on the role of the Vandeleur landlord family in the establishment of the town, their record during the Great Famine of 1847 and their international fame from the 1888 Vandeleur Evictions. The centre is also the starting point of the Kilrush Heritage Trail, through the landlord planned streets of Kilrush.

SCATTERY ISLAND

Scattery Island, to the south of Kilrush, is a twenty-minute boat journey from Cappa Pier. According to the Annals of the Four Masters, the island is referred to as Inis-Cathaigh (the Island of the Monster). The Cathach means the Battler and refers to a monster or demon that took over the island. Local legend has it that Saint Senan who was born in the area in around the year 500, came to the island and cast out the monster and freed the people. In the sixth century Saint Senan established a monastic settlement and place of study there that was highly regarded. Records show that in 563 fifty students and seminarians travelled from the continent to Ireland and divided into five groups and enrolled in various monasteries. One group went to study and pray on Scattery Island. When Saint Senan died he was buried in the monastery. During his lifetime females were forbidden to inhabit the island.

At one period there were reputed to have been eleven churches on this early Christian monastic site. There are presently the ruins of six churches and a round tower, about eighty feet high, with a conical stone roof and a doorway at ground level. The most interesting building is the Romanesque cathedral, east of the tower.

The wealth of the monastic sites on Scattery Island meant that it was raided several times by the Vikings. Because of the isolated location and strategic position on the River Shannon, Scattery became a small settlement for the Vikings based in Limerick. As many of them had converted to Christianity they established their own small community on the island.

In 970 Brian Boru, with the support of some other clans, recaptured Scattery Island and killed all the inhabitants numbering over 600. In 1188, following the death of the bishop of Scattery Island, the area of the island was combined with the parish of Killaloe. This was the last bishop of Scattery Island.

In September 1588 the *Annunciado* of the Spanish Armada, was damaged off Scattery Island. Rather than let the vessel fall into enemy hands the crew salvaged the cargo and burned the ship. Her crew was rescued and stores were transferred onto other ships of the Armada. When the storm abated six other Armada ships that had sought refuge set sail for Spain.

From the late 1600s there was a lighthouse on the island and in 1872 a new lighthouse was erected that still stands today. There remain some deserted houses of the island's last inhabitants.

During the summer months boat trips are run to Scattery Island from Kilrush.

KILLIMER

The name Killimer in Irish is Cill Iomar, the Church of Iomar or Emer, a female saint. There is confusion and some believe that the saint associated with this area is Saint Imar. Close to Killimer there is a ring fort, Lisroe Fort.

In the small cemetery is the grave of Ellen Hanley who became known as the Colleen Bawn. A teacher, Peter O'Connell, who recovered her body from the River Shannon erected a monument to her and he is interred in the same grave himself. Ellen Hanley was the Colleen Bawn of Gerald Griffin's novel, Dion Boucicault's play and Benedict's opera *The Lily of Killarney*. The story is based on that of a woman, Ellen who was married to John Scanlon of Croom, County Limerick. He murdered her in a jealous rage and disposed of her body in the Shannon. Scanlon was hanged for the murder.

Terminus for the car-ferry at Killimer, c. 1996.

In 1968 the ESB established an electricity generating station on each side of the Shannon, one in Moneypoint. They are easily distinguishable by their giant twin chimneys.

A car ferry linking Killimer to Tarbert, County Kerry opened in May 1969. A traveller intending to go from Clare to Kerry can avoid Limerick city by taking the ferry. The first ferry on the service was *Shannon Heather* and a decade later *Shannon Willow* transported cars and passengers across the Shannon.

LOOP HEAD

The West Clare Peninsula and coastal drive is a long finger of rugged countryside that juts into the Atlantic Ocean. The coast lying south westwards from Kilkee, for about 15 miles, to Loop Head, has a succession of caverns, chasms, sea-stacks and unusual shaped rocks that have been sculpted and carved by the constant battering of the ocean. There are some small islands off the coast.

The best method of exploring the area to Loop Head is to travel from Kilkee to the village of Doonaha, Dún Átha, 'Fort of the Ford'. In 1796 the famous Irish scholar, Eugene O'Curry (Eoghan O Comhraidhe), was born in Doonaha. O'Curry was self-educated and joined the Ordnance Survey Office in 1834. He worked on cataloguing Irish manuscripts in the British Museum and then in Trinity College, Dublin and later the Royal Irish Academy. He was appointed to the chair of Irish History and Archaeology in the new University College, Dublin. O'Curry's many works of ancient Irish history and customs are valuable reference sources to this day as is his translation of *Ancient Laws of Ireland* in which he collaborated with John O'Donovan. O'Curry died in 1862.

Then proceed southwards to Carrigaholt, a small Irish-speaking village on the shore of the Shannon. The Irish college in Carrigaholt is named after Eugene O'Curry. The name Carrigaholt in Irish is Carraig an Cabhailtigh, 'Rock of the Fleet,' referring to the historic and strategic significance of the area. The large rock rises over the entrance to the harbour. The name was earlier referred to as Carrick an Oultagh, a corruption of the name and referring to a castle built by the MacMahon's in around 1480. In the fifteenth century the MacMahons built a tower beside the pier. In 1652 a Cromwellian force, led by General Ludlow, captured the castle. The castle was later taken over by Donal O'Brien who built the first pier there early in the seventeenth century. The most important member of this branch of the O'Briens was Lord Clare, who formed the famous Clare's Dragoons. He drilled them in the village of Carrigaholt, before leading them in the service of France at Fontenoy and other parts of France in the late seventeenth and eighteenth centuries.

Carrigaholt castle, c. 1950.

When, on Ramillies' bloody field,
The baffled French were forced to yield
The victor Saxon backward reeled
Before the charge of Clare's Dragoons.

Following the Williamite wars, Carrigaholt Castle and its lands were confiscated and granted to the Burton family. Within a short radius of Carrigaholt there are miles of unspoilt coastline and cliff-walks with good vantage points for bird watching. Among the species in the area are ravens, kittiwakes, sabine gulls and razorbills.

At Kilcredau point there is a fort that was erected at the beginning of the nineteenth century. This was one of a series of batteries erected from 1806 at the mouth of the Shannon as watch-towers in the event of a French invasion. In 1824 a lighthouse was erected on the headland. In 1947, a Greek steamship *Okeanos* ran onto the rocks here and sank.

Further west is the village of Kilbaha, Coill Beite, 'Church of the Birchwood,' with its small harbour. There was a period of unrest in the locality as two local landlords, Marcus and Henry Keane sought to convert peasants to Protestantism. These converts became known as 'soupers'. Kilbaha was to receive notoriety in the early 1850s when the parish priest of Moyarta, Father Michael Meehan came into conflict with the bigoted local landlord, Marcus Keane and his land agent. With no building to celebrate

Mass, Fr Meehan converted two houses into a church but brought on the wrath of Keane who evicted the priest and his congregation from the premises. The priest found another method of foiling the landlord by building a wooden shelter on wheels where Mass could be celebrated on the shore between tides. The structure became known as the Little Ark.

Another spectacular location is the Bridge of Ross, natural sea arches that have taken a severe battering from the sea and only one bridge now remains.

Three miles west a lighthouse marks Loop Head, the most westerly point on the peninsula where the Atlantic and Shannon estuary merge. An area of cliff off Loop Head is called 'Diarmuid and Grainne's Rock' and the intervening channel is known as 'The Lover's Leap'. According to legend, this is where Cuchulainn, while being pursued by the red-haired witch, Mal, leaped onto a rock but she missed the leap and fell into the sea. Her blood is said to have turned the sea red and she was swept northwards to a point near the Cliffs of Moher, named Hag's Head. Thereafter, the headland became known as Loop Head, in Irish, Leap Head.

Over the past four centuries there have been a variety of lighthouses erected on Loop head. With dangerous rock formations in the locality it was necessary to warn merchant and war ships of the impending danger. The original signal was a burning beacon and in the 1720s a form of lighthouse was erected here. It was a century later before a formal lighthouse with oil lamps and reflectors went into operation. In 1854 the present lighthouse, standing 277 feet was erected. In 1971 the system was electrified and automated two decades later.

A highly worthwhile trip is on the *Dolphin Watch* boat that takes passengers in search of Bottlenose Dolphins in the Shannon Estuary.

CRATLOE

A short distance out of Limerick on the Ennis Road is the border of County Clare. The Cratloe Hills form a boundary between Limerick and Killaloe. Cratloe in Irish is Creatralac, 'A Place of Sally Trees,' an area once famous for its woods. The roof of Westminister Hall in London, Aileach Palace, Derry, and the Amsterdam City Hall (now the Royal Palace) were made from the great oaks that cover Woodcock Hill that rises behind the ruined castle. The woods were once the haunt of Freeney, a legendary highwayman. Regularly he held up mail coaches and wealthy travellers en route to Ennis.

In 1215 Geoffrey Lutteral was granted 'the land of Cratelralac (Cratloe) for thirty ounces of gold.' Shane MacNamara built the sturdy Cratloe Castle in the fifteenth century, a fine example of the many castles that are dotted all over County Clare. In 1584 the castle was under the control of Donal Mac Teige MacNamara. The following year the castle and 360 acres were transferred to Edward White, Clerk of the Connaught Council. At Saint John's Well nearby, annual patterns were held on the saint's feast day and attracted huge crowds. The church ruins are also believed to have associations with the saint.

In 1715 the great poet, Denis MacNamara 'Ruadh', was born in the district. In 1764 he converted to the Established Church of Ireland. One of his works was Ban Chnoic Eireann Oigh. In 1846 Ballymorris House was erected less than a mile south-west of Cratloe, on the site of an earlier fort built by a Danish chieftain named Maurice, after whom the building was named.

On 20 January 1920, a group of Irish Volunteers ambushed an RIC patrol at Meelick, near Cratloe, shooting dead two policemen.

BUNRATTY

The small village of Bunratty is on the N18, Limerick to Ennis Road. One of the most striking features of the village is the bulk of Bunratty Castle that towers over the river of the same name. The river is also known as the Owenogarney. The name Bunratty in Irish is Bun Rataigh, 'The Foot of the Ratty.' The castle is the fourth of that name and is more than four centuries old. At each corner there is a tower with six rooms.

Bunratty Castle, c. 1954.

The Vikings were first to appreciate the importance of the location and also built a fort here.

In 1248 King Henry III granted the lands of Tradaree in South Clare to the Norman knight, Robert de Muscegros ordering him to fortify the area. Consequently he built the first castle at Bunratty in wood, strategically guarding the Bunratty River. De Muscegros was granted permission to cut down oak trees for the erection of a castle on the site in a motte-and-bailey style. In 1276 de Muscegros surrendered his lands to the King who granted the castle to Sir Thomas de Clare, the youngest son of the Duke of Glouchester. He reinforced the building in stone. For many years the Clare's were engaged in a struggle with the O'Briens over control in Munster. Thomas's son, Richard de Clare and grandson were killed at the Battle of Dysert O'Dea in 1318. His wife, on hearing the news burned the castle and fled to England. In 1353, Thomas de Rokeby completely rebuilt the castle in stone but soon afterwards it was destroyed again.

Some sections of the present building date to the mid-fifteenth century when the MacNamaras were in control. The present castle dates to 1425. By 1500 the O'Briens occupied the castle. In 1543 King Henry VIII appointed the owner, Murrough O'Brien, First Earl of Thomond.

In 1646 Vice-Admiral William Penn arrived in Ireland with 700 troops and a small fleet, with orders to capture Bunratty Castle from the Confederate army. He was successful and held the castle. In 1641 his wife's property had been confiscated and

Cromwell compensated Penn with other allocations of land. Sir William was father of William Penn, the Quaker, who founded Pennsylvania in the United States. As a child Sir William Penn lived in Bunratty with his family. The Stoddert family later purchased the castle.

Thomas Amory was born in Bunratty in 1691. He became noted as the author of two extraordinary biographical works 'Memoirs' containing the *Lives of Several Ladies of Great Britain* and *The Life of John Buncle*.

John Scott Vandaleur, an Irish landlord, had two estates in County Clare; one, comprising 700 acres, was tenanted, but the second, of 618 acres at Ralahine, near Bunratty was farmed in a progressive fashion by Vandaleur himself. Vandaleur, who lived in a fine mansion beside Bunratty, was enthusiastic about the possibility of forming a village of co-operation, on the lines advocated by Robert Owens, regarded as the father of co-operation. Vandaleur stated that a mutual co-operative would lead to increased productivity and improve conditions between landlord and workers, but his family was not impressed. They believed that the tenant and labouring classes should be kept strictly in their place.

In 1830 Vandaleur began the first steps of his co-operative village by building a row of stone cottages, dormitories for single men and women, a store, a school, a large dining room and a meeting room. Around this period the atmosphere became so

Bunratty Castle, 2004.

Folk Village, Bunratty, 2004.

volatile that Clare magistrates had to request Dublin Castle to send reinforcements to suppress the armed peasants who were attempting to terrorise landlords into reducing rents. Vandaleur's steward, Daniel Hastings, was despised for his inhumane methods. In retaliation one of the labourers shot Hastings dead. Vandaleur left for Manchester but encouraged Edward Craig, an expert on the co-operative system, to return to Ralahide to organise a similar project there. Despite the troubled climate Craig organised a meeting in November 1831 for labourers, artisans and servants, as a result of which the Ralahine Agricultural and Manufacturing Co-Operative Association was formed. In time Ralahine proved a most successful enterprise and the co-operative movement spread throughout the country.

In 1804 Bunratty House was built as a temporary residence for the family who lived in Bunratty Castle. The family found the modern residence more to their liking and they never moved back to the castle.

In June 1919 a British Brigadier, General Lucas, was captured and handed over to some local Volunteers near Bunratty, under the control of Michael Brennan.

Following many decades of neglect, Lord Gort purchased Bunratty Castle and in conjunction with Bord Failte and the Office of Public Works initiated, in 1954, a major restoration of the building. After much refurbishment Bunratty Castle regained its former splendour with fifteenth- and sixteenth-century furniture, rich tapestries, old armour and portraits of former residents hanging on the walls.

Today, on summer nights, guests can attend medieval banquets in the castle where girls in sixteenth-century gowns serve mull and food and the Bunratty Singers entertain the guests.

Bunratty Folk Park is within the grounds of the castle where Irish village life at the turn of the century is recreated. The Folk Park contains typical nineteenth-century rural and urban houses. There are eight farmhouses, a watermill, a forge, a village street with a pub, post office, printers, pawnshop, hotel, school, drapery and hardware shops. The visitor can watch traditional skills such as pottery, weaving, knitting, bread-making and photography in their natural setting. MacNamara's village pub is an exact copy of the original Kearney's Hotel in Ennis with most of the furnishings and fittings from the original hotel in situ. In 1994 scenes for the television production of *The Old Curiosity Shop*, starring Peter Ustinov, were filmed in the Folk Park.

SHANNON

Shannon and Shannon Airport are south-east of Ennis, off the main road to Limerick. The airport is situated on a townland close to the estuary of the River Fergus. The airport was the first custom-free airport and is now also the site of a large industrial estate and the centre of Ireland's aerospace industry. The name Shannon in Irish is An tSionna, meaning 'The Old One.' Ptolemy recorded the name in the second

Shannon Airport, c. 1954.

century AD as Senos. Shannon is the newest town in Clare and grew up around the site of the airport.

There is evidence that people from the Neolithic period lived in this area and excavations have uncovered ring forts and other artefacts dating to the Bronze Age. A stone axe was discovered at Tullyglass. In the sixth century Saint Senan exiled Saint Conaire from Scattery Island and she is believed to have founded a church here. It is reputed that Saint Senan founded a church on Feenish Island.

One of the most famous people to have associations with the area was Robert Clive who became known as Clive of India. Following the battle of Plassey in 1757 Clive was awarded the title Baron Clive of Plassey, County Clare. He bought extensive property in the area including Rineanna and several houses.

From 1929 the possibility of a transatlantic service was under serious consideration by the Irish government. In 1936, after years of speculation, the government announced that it had chosen a site. The area finally chosen for the aerodrome was a 760-acre open marsh at Rineanna, meaning a Place on the Marsh. In 1937 work commenced on the site but was interrupted by the Second World War. During the emergencies of 1939-45, the Air Corps established a permanent base at the airport.

It was 1942 before a serviceable airport was established but it took three further years before the first scheduled commercial flight passed through Shannon – a Douglas DC 4 owned by American Overseas Airways. That same year, Pan Am, TWA and BOAC (now British Airways) also began flights through Shannon. Soon Sabena, Air France

A Shannon Farmhouse.

and KLM were using the airport as well. Before long Shannon gained a reputation as the gateway between Europe and America and the number of international carriers using it, grew steadily in the coming years. At that time, limited aircraft range meant that journeys had to be broken for refuelling and Shannon was ideally placed to capitalise on this.

In 1947 Shannon became the world's first Custom Free Airport, from which shops were opened and a mail order company was established. The Shannon Free Airport Development Authority was to create an industrial estate in the vicinity of the airport. Incentives were given to attract foreign companies with grants to build factories and a ten-year free profit scheme. The Shannon scheme was successful in attracting firms from the USA, England, Germany and Japan, providing thousands of jobs in the industrial estate. The development co-built a housing estate on Drumgeely Hill to accommodate the workers. From the beginning, the town of Shannon expanded rapidly and has developed into one of the largest towns in County Clare, with a population of almost 10,000.

In 1951 Sean Lemass appointed Clare-born Brendan O'Regan, as Controller of Sales and Catering at Shannon. The operation was an immediate success and led to the founding of Shannon Free Airport Development Authority. O'Regan was also responsible for establishing the Shannon College of Hotel Management that trained graduates for key positions in the hotel industry. The college gained status and is regarded as the premier institution in this field.

In the late 1950s Shannon Airport experienced difficulties but the arrival of the Dublin-Shannon-New York connection, was to ease the pressure. In the early days the Department of Industry and Commerce ran Shannon Airport but in 1969 Aer Rianta took control of the airport management.

In 1975 Guinness Peat Aviation (GPA), the aircraft brokerage firm, began operations at Shannon. In 1981 a group of residents at Shannon, met to seek Town Commissioner status for the area. On 1 January, the following year, Shannon Town Commissioners was established.

Down through the years many distinguished figures have stopped off at Shannon Airport, including Marlene Dietrich, John Wayne, Danny Kaye, Charlie Chaplin, Greta Garbo, Marlon Brando and James Cagney. Many world leaders have stopped at Shannon including Fiedel Castro, John Foster Dulles, Anthony Eden and Mikhail Gorbachev. Since 1945 practically all the United States Presidents have visited Shannon, from Harry Truman, Dwight Eisenhower, John F. Kennedy, Lyndon Johnson, Richard Nixon, Gerald Ford, Jimmy Carter, Ronald Reagan to George Bush, Bill Clinton and George W. Bush. On 1 October 1979, Pope John Paul II left Shannon after his historical visit to Ireland. In September 1994 Boris Yeltsin never left his plane at Shannon when he arrived to meet Taoiseach Albert Reynolds and his ministers, who were waiting on the runway.

In 1984 there was increased business at Shannon with Aeroflot, the Soviet airline, using the airport for the transfer of passengers on the New York-Moscow flights. Since 1990 there have been fears for the future of the airport with the Shannon stop-over becoming a controversial issue. Over the years Shannon has been the focus of many protests, the most recent being in 2003 when protesters objected to the airport being used as a stop-off zone for American troops bound for the war in Iraq.

NEWMARKET-ON-FERGUS

Newmarket-on-Fergus is a medium-sized town on the N18 road from Ennis to Limerick, about 6 miles north of Shannon Airport. The town takes its name from a nineteenth-century O'Brien, Lord Inchiquin, who was fond of horses. Formerly the village was known as Kilnasoolagh but was changed to its present name by the renowned horse owner and breeder, Sir Edward O'Brien (1705-65), after the English racing venue.

He was extravagant with money and erected the small hilltop building opposite the entrance to Dromoland Castle, 2½ miles north of the town. This structure served as his stand for observing his racehorses in training.

The name Newmarket-on-Fergus in Irish is Cora Chaitlin, 'Kathleen's Weir'. The Gaelic name refers to a member of the family who constructed the weir. There are many castles and church ruins in the vicinity of Newmarket-on-Fergus,

A folly at Newmarket-on-Fergus.

the most interesting being Urlanmore Castle, 2 miles south-west, and the fifteenth-century Drimcastle.

The best-known castle in the district is Dromoland Castle, one of the most 'baronial' castles on the west coast. The castle was the seat of Lord Inchiquin, a direct descendant of Brian Boru, High King of Ireland in the tenth century. In 1685 the O'Briens from Leamaneh Castle completely moved to Dromoland and Donough O'Brien had the castle completely refurbished. The present castle was built in 1835 to the design of James and George Richard Pain, on the site of the earlier building overlooking Dromoland Lake and its large demesne. In the grounds of the castle is Moohaun (or Mooghaun) Fort, Mucan, 'A Heap of Stones', one of the largest hill forts in Ireland, enclosing 27 acres with three great stone walls, oval in outline. Close to the south-west entrance of the middle rampart there is a small ringfort.

In 1847 the first Irish-bred horse to win the Aintree Grand National, *Matthew*, was trained at Coolreagh, Bodyke.

The Dromoland O'Briens are buried in the Church of Ireland church of Kilnasoolagh, where there is an impressive marble effigy of Sir Donough O'Brien. In 1962, an American, Bernard McDonough bought the castle. Today Dromoland Castle operates as a luxury hotel.

In 1803 William Smith O'Brien, Leader of the Young Irelanders, was born in Newmarket-on-Fergus. In 1854 workmen digging a railway line in the area discovered a hoard of gold ornaments. Some of the pieces were melted down but the surviving ones were presented to the National Museum in Dublin. The discovery became known as the Great Clare Gold Find.

CLARECASTLE

The village of Clarecastle is located where the Ennis Road crosses the River Fergus estuary which is navigable to this juncture. Clarecastle was once known as Clare and takes its name from a castle commanding the river crossing. This O'Brien castle that was once occupied by the Earl of Thomond is believed to have given its name to County Clare when it was created a county in 1576. Clarecastle in Irish is An Clar indicating a 'Board on the Ford.'

In 1248 King Henry III granted tracts of land in the area to the Norman knight, Robert de Muscegros, who built a castle, at a strategic location, blocking the entrance to the River Fergus and access to Clonroad, stronghold of the O'Briens. Like most Norman castles a community grew up around it and fairs were held there regularly.

When Conor O'Brien died, his successor, Brian Rua, destroyed Clare Castle and re-established the O'Briens in the territory of Tradraige. In 1570, a descendant, another Conor O'Brien of Clarecastle was summoned by the English authorities

An antique shop in Clarecastle, c. 1996.

to the assizes in Ennis but he refused to attend. Troops under the control of his uncle, Sir Donal of Ennistymon, were despatched to Clarecastle but Conor attacked them and held them prisoners at the castle. As a result of this and other skirmishes with the forces of the Crown, Conor was forced to give up the castle and fled to the continent.

About a mile north of the village, there are the ruins of Clare Abbey, founded in 1189 by King Donal Mor O'Brien, King of Limerick, for the Canons Regular of Saint Augustine. In 1650 Cromwellian forces attacked the priory, causing severe damage. Between the church and the lake is the Holy Well that pilgrims visited annually on 24 June. The remains of the abbey are largely fifteenth-century but include some early thirteenth-century work. At the Dissolution of the monasteries, the priory and its possessions were among the properties granted to Donnchada O'Brien, Baron of Ibracken, on condition that he gave up the name of O'Brien and undertook to use English mannerisms, customs and dress. Donnchada disputed the kingship of Thomond with Turlough O'Brien and as a compromise the area was divided amongst the two men. Donnchada took charge of the eastern section of Thomond and Turlough the remainder. In 1283 Donnchadh was drowned in the River Fergus and Turlough became king of all Thomond.

In 1773, the great bridge builder, John Semple, constructed a five-arch bridge over the River Fergus to replace an earlier structure. Two centuries later, in 1973 the present bridge was built.

From the early 1790s when France declared war on Britain there were fears of a French invasion of Ireland. As a precaution a militia act for Ireland was passed. The militia served as an auxiliary force to support the regular army. In May 1793 the Clare militia was formed and its headquarters was at the castle in Clarecastle. They frequently marched and drilled in the village giving pleasure to the locals. With the force being billeted there, business proved lucrative for the traders in the area.

In 1847 Clarecastle experienced a serious outbreak of cholera with many deaths. From the mid-1800s cargo boats arrived in Clarecastle carrying coal and timber for merchants in Ennis. In the 1940s and '50s coal was hauled from Clarecastle to Ennis with Shire horses pulling the carts. In the 1960s tidal barriers were erected on the river that resulted in lowering water levels in Ennis during high tides that previously caused frequent flooding.

Carnelly House, built in the eighteenth century with Dutch blocks, to a design of Francis Bindon, is regarded as one of the earliest Georgian houses in County Clare. For a time the Lord Chief Justice of Ireland, Peter O'Brien, resided there.

Other places of note in the locality include a number of small caves around Killone. The Catholic church has a window by Michael Healy, 'Christ Carrying Cross,' erected in 1927.

QUIN

The small village of Quin, is on the road between Newmarket-on-Fergus and Crusheen, on the River Rine, in Irish Aba na Rinne, 'The River of the Point.' The name Quin in Irish is Cuince, 'The Arbutus Grove' or 'Quince Tree.'

In 1278 Richard de Clare built Quin Castle and for a period it became the centre of Norman power in the region. The village developed around the castle and Saint Finghin's church. In 1318 following their victory at Dysert O'Dea, the O'Briens captured the castle but some years later the castle was attacked and burned by the MacNamaras.

The village has one of the best preserved monastic ruins in Ireland, Quin Abbey, a Franciscan friary founded in 1350 by the MacNamaras, Lords of Clancullen. The abbey incorporated part of the original structure built by Richard de Clare. Later the building was greatly enlarged by Maccon MacNamra. In 1541 Lord Deputy Perrot executed Donough O'Brien at the friary. That same year the friary was suppressed but the monks soon returned and the last member of the community, Friar John Cogan, died in 1820 and is buried in the cloisters. A famous duellist named Fireballs MacNamara is also buried in the friary. Many of the tombs within the ruins are well preserved.

Quin Abbey, a former Franciscan friary, c. 1992.

The old RIC barracks in Quin.

In 1650 a skirmish took place at Quin between Clare clansmen brought together by the Irish bishops, including John O'Mahony, Bishop of Killaloe and Colonel Wogan of Ormonde's Army. They all fought together against General Ireton and his Cromwellian force.

Magh Adhair, the burial mound of Adhar, the last of the Fir Bolg chieftains is situated at Quin. The chieftains of Dal gCais gathered there regularly for the inauguration of the Kings of Thomond. South of Quin is Moghane Hill-Fort, a stone ring-fort, approximately 85 feet in diameter and about 6 feet high with a single entrance.

According to the census of 1831 the village had a population of 173 and 24 houses. In the *Parliamentary Gazette* of 1845 Quin was described as 'a wretched collection of poor cabins, but contains the modern and substantial, though plain church and Roman Chapel of the Parish'. In 1840 there were lead mines on the lands of Hugh Singleton where men and women worked in deplorable conditions. There were small farming units in the community in which small tenant farmers eked out a living. Another enterprise in the locality was seaweed which was brought up along the River Fergus to Latoon, 3 miles from the village, for fertilising the soil. Quin RIC barracks was built in 1848.

Bronze Age man was constantly under attack by rebel tribes and as a means of creating a defence some of them built their homes on a lake. One of the best known of these was the 'crannog' or lake dwelling. They were simple dwellings made from reeds, wattles and mud and communities varied from around six dwellings to extensive

The old RIC barracks in Quin today.

enclosures containing many more. Within the compound there was a communal cooking area known as a fulacht fiadh.

About 3 miles from Quin is Knappogue Castle built in 1467 by the MacNamaras. In 1649 Cromwellian troops captured and occupied the castle. In later years, the large medieval tower house had sections added by the Scott family of Cahincon. In around 1855 Theobald Butler, Baron Dunboyne, bought the castle and restored it.

In the War of Independence the East Clare Flying Column of the IRA were based in Knappogue Castle. In 1966 the castle was purchased by Mark Edwin Andrews from Texas, USA and developed as a tourist attraction. Nightly during the summer season there is a medieval banquet, a good-humoured evening with fine food and entertainment recalling the area's Celtic past. There is also an audio-visual display and craft shop at the castle.

Craggaunowen Castle was built near Quin in the sixteenth century as a MacNamara tower house. The ancient castle later came under the control of Thomas Steele of Cullaun House, who renovated the building. Later the castle was taken over by the Land Commission and in 1965 art historian John Hunt purchased the property that now contains a number of objects from his collection of medieval art. He undertook a major project that became known as Craggaunowen Bronze Age Project that involved restoration of the castle and creating a crannog complete with a ring fort, crannogs and an underground chamber. Also on display is the hide boat *The Brendan* in which Tim Severin sailed from Ireland to the United States in 1976-7, re-enacting the voyage of Saint Brendan, reputed to have discovered America before Columbus.

Within a short radius of Quin there are the ruins of a number of castles including Corbally, Crevagh, Ballymarkhan and Danganbrack. In the early nineteenth century the Earl of Thomond built Ballykilty House. Saint Finghin's church, south of Quin, was built at the end of the thirteenth century but only the ruin remains today.

ENNIS

Ennis, the capital of County Clare, is ideally situated in the centre of the county, on a bend of the River Fergus, on the main Limerick-Galway road. The town is the centre of administration, commerce and industry for the county. As early as the reign of Queen Elizabeth I the town had been established as the county town. The town's narrow streets and market square are steeped in history and have strong political associations recalling the monster political rallies of Daniel O'Connell, Charles Stewart Parnell and Eamon de Valera. The name Ennis in Irish is Inis, 'River Meadow'.

In 1242 the king of Thomond, Donnchada Cairbreach O'Brien, invited the Franciscans to the town to establish a friary, close to the bridge over the River Fergus. The Franciscans dually accepted and built the friary. Within a short period, a settlement developed around it and the area became known as the Island of the Son of Ineall. Nearby the O'Briens also created a settlement known by several names including the Island of Streams. In time the two settlements were connected and became the town of Ennis.

Ennis came into prominence in the sixteenth century as the county town of Clare. In 1297 eleven other counties were officially recognised and 'shired'. There were many attempts to shire Clare and it was not until Conor O'Brien reached a settlement with the authorities over his property at Clarecastle that Sir Henry Sidney declared Clare a county. Finally in 1576 Clare was established as a county with Ennis as its capital. In 1609 King James I granted permission to hold fairs and markets in the town. Large markets were held on listed days throughout the year. In 1612 Ennis was created a borough and by 1680 the town had 120 houses and 600 inhabitants. Twenty of the houses were slated, the remainder thatched.

For a long period the Franscian friary was a seat of learning and attracted students from across Europe. In 1651 the monks were forcibly removed by Cromwellian troops but returned some years later.

In 1790 the first theatre was opened in Clare in Cook's Lane. In the mid-nineteenth century large numbers of poor people lived in cabins on the approach roads to the town. In 1846 the *Parliamentary Gazette* of Ireland gave the following description: 'The town itself, in spite of having some good houses in the interior and several neat villas on its outskirts, presents a very shabby and even poor and disorderly appearance. The streets are in general narrow, crooked, irregularly edificed and without any feasible claim to cleanliness or comfort.'

Ennis Friary, founded in 1240 by Donncadh Cairbreach O'Brien, King of Thomond.

River Fergus, Ennis.

During this period there was also considerable growth and prosperity in the town. In 1831 work commenced on the Pro-Cathedral of Saints Peter and Paul, to a design by Dominic Madden but was not completed until four decades later. In the 1850s the Convent of Mercy and the Courthouse, a fine example of classic revival architecture, were completed. In 1856 the Presbyterian church, now the de Valera Museum and Library, was built at a cost of £570. In the 1870s the Church of Ireland church and the asylum were completed. Saint Flannan's College, designed by Frank O'Connor, was built of limestone between 1879-81.

In O'Connell Square, in the town centre, there is a monument to Daniel O'Connell, at the place of the great meeting to nominate him as the representative of Ennis in the English Parliament. In June 1828 when the election was pending, the Catholic Association was determined to find a strong candidate to stand against the sitting MP,

O'Connell monument, Ennis.

Vesey Fitzgerald, who was appointed to the Board of Trade in the British cabinet. There was a ground swell of support for O'Connell to stand and with less than a week to polling day he allowed his name to go forward. Feelings ran high in Ennis as supporters of the Catholic Association came into conflict with the landed gentry and additional troops had to be drafted in to maintain order. Priests canvassed support for O'Connell off the altar and small farmers and tenants supported en masse. On polling day priests led their congregations to the polling booths. O'Connell had a resounding victory in the election and less than a year later Catholic Emancipation was granted by the British Parliament. In February 1830 O'Connell finally took his seat in the House of Commons not only as a member for Clare but also as the leader of a national movement. In August that year on the death of King George IV, a general election was called and O'Connell decided to leave his seat and stand in Waterford. In 1867 a 74-feet high doric column made by James Cahill was erected to Daniel O'Connell by public subscription on the site where he had been declared an MP for Clare.

The prolific Thomas Ennis Steele, a Protestant landlord, was Head Pacificator of Daniel O'Connell's Catholic Association. He was also an inventor of underwater equipment including a diving bell and harness. He brought the stone believed to mark the centre of Ireland from Birr to Cullane where O'Connell often stayed.

In 1880 Charles Stewart Parnell addressed one of the most important meetings of his career in Ennis. He advised farmers not to pay unjust rents and not to bid for farms from which others had been evicted. Anyone who broke this code should be placed in 'moral Coventry' and shunned by his neighbours. Parnell was arrested for his involvement with the Land League and imprisoned.

It was around this time that Parnell met Captain William O'Shea, the husband of Katharine O'Shea. William O'Shea was returned as a Member of Parliament for Clare for the Irish Party but he was an absentee landlord and a poor representative for his constituents and the local branch of the National League passed a motion of no confidence in him. From an early stage O'Shea became aware of his wife's affair with Parnell whom he challenged to a duel that never materialised. Some years later O'Shea was to be the architect of Parnell's downfall when he cited him as co-respondent in his divorce case. Following the divorce Parnell married Katharine but there was a rapid decline in his health, and he died in Brighton in October 1891, aged forty-five.

In 1880 a major land reclamation scheme was initiated in Ennis in which a large stone causeway from the mainland made Islandavanna a peninsula. The project provided major employment in the area and over 400 labourers were recruited. In 1880 the jail was built in the town, the site of which is now occupied by The Old Ground Hotel.

Many killings occurred in County Clare during the 1916-23 period. In April 1922 an ex-RIC man was shot dead in the town. In April 1923 three Irregulars were convicted of killing a Free Stater and later executed in Home Barracks, Ennis, although they were innocent of the killing. They were the last men to be executed during this troubled period.

Also in Ennis there is a statue of Eamon de Valera, former Taoiseach and President of Ireland. He was born in New York on 14 October 1882 to an Irish immigrant mother and a Spanish immigrant father. In 1885 he moved to Ireland and became involved in the Republican movement. During the 1916 Rising he was a commandant of the force at Boland's Mill in Dublin. On being arrested he was sentenced to death, but the authorities commuted the death penalty as there was confusion about his nationality and they did not want to alienate the United States.

Statue of Eamon de Valera, Ennis.

Following the death of Major William Redmond, who had represented East Clare as MP at Westminster for over twenty-five years, de Valera was approached to stand for the constituency. His election poster read:

> *Of American-Irish Spanish*
> *De Valera spat in England's face,*
> *The gap of danger's still his place*
> *To lead historic Clare's Dragoons.*
> *Viva la for Ireland's wrong !*
> *Viva la for Ireland's right !*
> *Viva la in Sinn Féin throng,*
> *For a Spanish steed and sabre bright !*

In 1917 de Valera had a decisive victory with 5,010 votes against 2,035 for Patrick Lynch and was elected as a Sinn Féin MP for East Clare. He was to retain this seat in the Dail from 1917 to 1959 when he was elected third President of Ireland.

On Sunday 30 April 1921 a pro-treaty meeting was held in the town at which Michael Collins was the main speaker. In July 1921 the river bridge over the Erinagh River was blown up between Corofin and Ennis and in April 1922 an RIC sergeant was shot dead in Ennis. Many executions were carried out in the old Home Barracks in Kilrush Road. On 15 August 1923 at a Sinn Féin rally Eamon de Valera was arrested by the military and taken to the barracks. When the troops appeared there was a stampede and hundreds of people were injured. In the election on 27 August de Valera headed the poll, while he was in Arbour Hill prison. Following his release from prison the following year he returned to Clare amid bonfires and great celebrations. 'Dev' addressed many major political rallies in Ennis.

A number of other prominent people have had connections with Ennis. In 1775 the poet, Thomas Dermody, was born there. He was the son of an Ennis teacher and his best-known work was *The Harp of Erin*. William Mulready, the son of a breeches maker, was born in Ennis in 1786. He became one of the most renowned painters of his era and he designed the first five-penny postage envelope issued by Rowland Hill, the organiser of the penny post. He died in 1863.

The actor-manager, Walter Smithson lived in Ennis where he opened the New Theatre in 1790. He ran many seasons of popular plays in the town. Later he opened several more theatres in the south of the country. In 1800 he ran a benefit performance of *Romeo and Juliet* for his actress wife. Several months later his daughter, Harriett Constance Smithson was born in Ennis. She was adopted and reared by the Rector of Ennis, Dr James Barrett. She followed the family tradition and became a gifted actress and later toured through Europe with many productions. She married Hector Berlioz, the great French composer and spent her later life in Paris where she died and was buried in 1854.

A ruined castle near Ennis.

One of the most impressive buildings in Ennis is the courthouse, built in 1838 to a design by Henry Whitestone. A Russian cannon from the Crimean War is located in front of the building. In 1881 the Maid of Erin statue was erected to commemorate three Irish Nationalists executed in Manchester in 1867.

In 1858-59 the railway line was extended from Limerick to Ennis and added enormously to the prosperity of the town. It was a decade later before the renowned West Clare Railway opened and Ennis became the headquarters of the two railway lines. The total length of the two systems was 53 miles, comprising the main line from Ennis to Kilkee (48 miles) and a branch line from Moyasta Junction to Kilrush and Cappa Pier (5 miles). In 1960 Coras Iompar Eireann closed the line and the tracks of the West Clare Railway were ripped up and sold to Nigeria.

In 1956, a floor of Carmody's Hotel in Abbey Street collapsed while an auction was in progress and eight people were killed and many more were injured.

One mile east of the left bank of the River Fergus, is the ancient church of Doora. Two miles north-west of Ennis, off the Corofin Road is Drumcliff church that was established in the sixth century. In the fifteenth century Drumcliff church was renovated partly with stone from the original building. In 1180 King Donal Mor O'Brien founded Killone Abbey, an Augustinian priory dedicated to Saint John, 4 miles south-west of Ennis, in the grounds of Newhall House. The house was the home of the McDonnells. According to legend, the nearby lake turned red, forecasting the death of a member of the family. This tale came from the legend of the killing of a mermaid in the lake by Newhall Butler, who had caught her stealing from the cellar and her blood had turned the lake red.

Although an old town, with narrow winding streets, indicating its medieval origin and traditional shop fronts, Ennis is a progressive business and market centre. There is a wide-ranging selection of amenities including an 18-hole golf course, a tennis court, and heated swimming pool. There is excellent coarse and brown trout fishing on the River Fergus and in the many lakes within the environs of the town. The Ennis Museum displays a wide variety of mementoes from the course of Irish history with a particular emphasis on local events. At the old railway station there is the preserved West Clare Railway engine, immortalised by Percy French in the famous song, 'Are ye right there, Michael, are ye right?' Comhaltas Ceoltóirí Éireann provides traditional music sessions throughout the year. A new addition to the town is the Glor International Music Centre.

The church buildings dominate the town. The Pro-Cathedral dedicated to Saints Peter and Paul was built in 1842 at a cost of £5,000. Its most impressive feature is its 170 feet spire. The church was renovated in 1911. Saint Flannan's College and the old Saint Mary's Franciscan Friary are other important landmarks. The main attractions of the friary are the carvings, with the McMahon tomb perhaps the best example. The nave and chancel are the oldest parts of the friary with the transept, sacristy and tower dating from the late fifteenth century.

In 1975 the old Presbyterian church won a European Architectural Heritage Year Award.

In September 1997 Ennis was chosen as the Information Age Town which has involved it in becoming the testing ground for new communications technology.

SPANCILHILL

The village of Spancilhill is to the east of Ennis on the Scarriff Road. The name in Irish is Cnoc Fhuarcoill, the Hill of the Cold Wood.

The village is best known as the location of the famous song, Spancilhill, written by Michael Considine. A Clare man, Considine emigrated to Canada in 1870 to seek his fortune. His intention was to save money and marry his girl friend, Mary MacNamara. Unfortunately luck was not on his side and he became ill. He feared that he was near death and wrote a poem that he sent home to his nephew, John. Music was put to the words and the singer Robbie McMahon made it a popular ballad.

An important feature of Spancilhill is the annual horse fair that attracts buyers and sellers from the surrounding counties. In 1621 the first charter to hold a fair was granted by King James I. These early fairs covered all types of livestock but later fairs were designated for donkeys, ponies and horses. At one stage the Spancilhill horse fair was the largest horse fair in the country and many horses for the army were purchased at the fair. It was always a custom for these fairs to take place where a number of roads merged.

COROFIN

Corofin is a small market village, on the Ennis to Kilfenora Road, lying between two lakes, the Inchiquin and Atedaun. The road from Ennistymon to Corofin runs parallel to the line of the old West Clare Railway, celebrated in song and story by Percy French. The name Corofin in Irish is Coradh Finne, 'the Weir of Finn.'

The area, known as the Lakelands of North Clare, has several excellent fishing lakes in the parishes of Corofin, Tubber and Ruan. Fishing is particularly good on Lough Inchiquin that is flanked on the west by a range of wooded hills. On the northern shore of Lough Inchiquin there is the ruin of Inchiquin Castle, erected in 1459. For many decades it was the seat of a branch of the O'Briens.

Corofin is at the entrance to the Burren and the Burren National Park at Mullaghmore. To the east of Lough Inchiquin the road runs northwards to Killinaboy where a twelve-foot stump of a round tower stands in the graveyard. The round tower was built in the early twelfth century. The towers were not places of refuge as sometimes believed but bell towers used to call monks and people from the surrounding countryside to prayer.

Just off the road from Corofin to Kilfenora is the ruined church of Kilnaboy. The name in Irish is Cill Ingheen Bhuidhe, meaning the Church of the Daughter of Baothi. She was a saint from the seventh century and the church is believed to date from this period. The original church is also reputed to have been associated with clan Ifernain, one of the migrant tribes of the Ui Fidgeinte, who settled in mid-Clare before the Dalcassians. The present church was built in the sixteenth century on the site of this earlier site. There are three holy wells within the environs of the village – Ballard, Anneville and Killinaboy.

Three miles south of Corofin is Dysert O'Dea, the location of an early church founded by Saint Tola of Clonard in the seventh century. On 10 May 1318 the famous Battle of Dysert O'Dea was fought at this juncture. The Norman knight, Richard de Clare, marched into Thomond at the head of a strong force. He split his army into three groups as they set about routing the O'Deas. The King of Thomond, Muircheartach O'Brien devised a plan to defeat Clare's force. When the Normans pursued a group of Conor O'Dea's clansmen rounding up livestock, the opposing forces met at the ford of Ballycullen where the battle began. Murtag O'Brien arrived with reinforcements and the Anglo-Normans took flight and ran into an ambush. Conor O'Dea, chieftain of the O'Dea clan butchered them and De Clare himself was slain. This battle proved decisive in the history of County Clare and prevented an Anglo-Norman invasion of Clare. With the loss of their leader de Clare's troops were routed and it was not for two centuries that the English regained a strong foothold in the county.

Diarmaid O'Dea built Dysert O'Dea castle in around 1480. Over the next century the Earl of Ormonde recaptured the castle before it reverted back to another O'Dea, Domhnall Maoe. In 1651 following the capture of Limerick by Cromwellian troops a force took possession of Dysert O'Dea castle and occupied it for a number of years.

A quiet street in Corofin.

Dysert O'Dea castle, Corofin, c. 1910.

The ruins of Leamaneh castle, 2004.

The Dysert O'Dea Castle and Archaeology Centre afford visitors an insight into the history and archaeology of the area. There is a museum, photographic exhibitions and audio-visual show. On the ground floor there is an audio-visual presentation of local history and archaeology, giving a trail of twenty-five sites of interest nearby.

Corofin grew gradually but from the early nineteenth century it was firmly established as a market and post town with a population of almost 1,000 people, living mainly in small thatched dwellings and making a living from the land or by working on the estates of the gentry. There was extensive poverty in the district and under the Poor Relief (Ireland) Act (1838) a workhouse was built in Corofin. It was inundated with requests from peasants seeking entry. One of the cruellest aspects of the workhouse system was that family units were segregated on entry. There were separate wards for men and boys and women and girls and no further contact was permitted between them. All the inmates, who were dressed in uniforms, had to work. The females worked in the kitchen, washroom and infirmary and the males were employed breaking stones and other manual jobs. During the famine years various relief schemes were initiated in the district to assist the starving families.

Five miles north-west of Corofin there are several prehistoric tombs in Leana and Parknabinnia. Two miles north at Tully Common there is a cliff-top stone fort with three concentric ramparts. It is believed that livestock were held in the outer enclosure. In 1934 the fort was excavated by the Harvard Archaeological Expedition. Two miles south-east of Corofin there are the ruins of Rath church with a Romanesque doorway. The patron saint of the church is Saint Blathmac.

Leamaneh Castle built in around 1500, a ruined castle and manor house, is located at the junction of the Ballyvaughan, Corofin and Kilfenora roads. The original tower house at Leamaneh was constructed about 1480 by Turlough Donn, a king in the Kingdom of Thomond and was known as Leim an Eich, the Horse's Leap. In 1548, Murrough, son of Turlough Donn, was awarded the title First Earl of Thomond and Baron Inchiquin.

The most famous resident of Leamaneh was Máire Rua MacMahon. In 1639 following the death of her husband, Máire Rua married Conor O'Brien of Leamaneh Castle. In 1651 O'Brien led a force of troops against General Ludlow and a Cromwellian

Church of Ireland, Corofin.

force. There was a bloody battle in which O'Brien was killed. To protect her property Maire Rua married a Cromwellian officer, John Cooper. She married several times and gave birth to at least eight children. There were countless myths and legends about Maire Rua from having twelve lovers to marrying twenty four times. Upon her death, her son, Donough, inherited the estate. He resided there until 1685 when he moved to Dromoland Castle. Maire Rua died around this time.

Following the restoration the Viceroy, James Butler, Duke of Ormonde was one of the most powerful men in Ireland and restored property confiscated by Cromwell. One person to benefit from this was Donough O'Brien who married Butler's niece and was granted large tracts of land in the baronies of Inchiquin and Dromoland. King James II made O'Brien a baronet and he was appointed sheriff of Clare from 1695 to 1715. He also served as a Member of Parliament for Clare and at one stage was the richest commoner in the country.

In the early 1800s the Synges, a Protestant landlord family, took over Dysert O'Dea Castle and lands from the O'Deas. In 1823 Edward Synge, a fundamental Protestant took control of the property. His priority was to convert as many of his Catholic tenants as possible to Protestantism. He used various, and dubious, methods to entice families to convert from building schools to offering inducements. The proud peasants showed strong opposition to his methods. In an ambush Synge's driver was shot dead but he escaped and thereafter toned down his proselytising.

In 1816 the painter and director of the National Gallery in London, Sir Frederick Burton, was born in Corofin House. He died in 1900. In the early nineteenth century the area experienced much bitterness between landlords and tenants who feared eviction due to arrears in rents. On 21 January 1831 a Resident Magistrate, William Blood, who lived at Applevale House, Corofin, was attacked and killed by a servant. There was immediate retribution by the authorities and eight local men were hanged at Corofin, Rath and Kilfenora.

In the early twentieth century, Powerstown House, south of the bridge over the River Fergus, served as an RIC barracks. In 1922 Free State troops planned to attack Corofin workhouse that was occupied by Irregulars. The latter were tipped off about the attack and burned the building before abandoning it.

The Clare Heritage Centre situated in the village is housed in a deconsecrated Church of Ireland church. This interpretative museum and genealogical research centre, portrays dramatic periods of Irish history from 1800-1860, under such headings as land tenure, traditional ways of life, culture, famine and emigration. The centre also houses comprehensive research material to enable people with County Clare roots to trace their ancestry. Also exhibited is an early Christian Tua cross and there is an index of all church records in the county.

CRUSHEEN

Crusheen, a hamlet in north Clare is on the main Gort to Ennis, N18 road. The name in Irish is Croisín, 'the Little Cross.'

Caheraphuc, a wedge tomb, south west of the village, is evidence of the existence of early inhabitants in the area. South of the village, on a peninsula in Inchicronan Lough, are the remains of a small Augustinian priory, successor of the first church founded by Saint Cronan (died 550) of Tuamgraney and a dependency of Clare Abbey in Clarecastle. The foundation of the priory is attributed to King Donal Mor O'Brien who built it for the Augustinian Canons of Clare. In 1615 the church was adapted for Protestant services by Donough O'Brien, Earl of Thomond.

At the neck of the peninsula are the ruins of the fifteenth-century Bryan's or O'Brien's Castle, a medieval tower house built by the clan. In 1651 the castle was the site of a battle in which the Cromwellian, General Ludlow, defeated a royalist force and Conor O'Brien, husband of Máire Rua of Leamaneh was killed.

The town prospered from the 1730s when permission was granted for the holding of a number of fairs annually. These attracted traders and merchants to the area.

Two miles west of Crusheen is Kiltoola church, now overgrown with ivy, close to the River Fergus and overlooking Dromore Wood. It is believed that Saint Tolga founded the church in the early thirteen century. There is the ruin of an old penal church at Kilvakee in Dromore Wood. In Crusheen parish there are two large boulders known as Coffin Rock and Hearse Stone.

The well-known story teller and writer, Eddie Lenihan, lives in Crusheen.

East Clare

MOUNTSHANNON

The picturesque village of Mountshannon is on the Portumna to Scarriff Road, situated in a prime location, on the shore of Lough Derg. The village is a favourite venue for a variety of pleasure craft and anglers, particularly during the mayfly season on the lake. The name Mountshannon in Irish is Baile Ui Bheolain, 'Boland's Town.'

Iniscealtra or Holy Island is located about one half mile offshore in Lough Derg. In 640 Saint Caimin founded a monastic settlement on the island. There are five ancient churches, a dry stone structure known as the Cottage, an unusual building called the Anochorities Cell that was used by early monks, a holy well and a 79 feet round tower. The church beside the round tower has a Hiberno-Romanesque chancel arch. There are still memorial stones in the saint's graveyard dating to between the eighth and twelfth centuries.

Due to its isolated and vulnerable location, Iniscealtra was attacked numerous times by the Vikings. The longships of the Vikings could navigate up rivers and launch raids on monasteries for their wealth. They were savage and would slaughter the monks at will. Despite the frequent attacks the monks remained there until the thirteenth century. For centuries the island was a popular place of pilgrimage and prayer. The festival at the holy well acquired an air of Bacchanalian revelry but was ended by the clergy when local squires attempted to procure the local girls.

Mountshannon that was developed in the eighteenth century, is a prime example of a landlord village. Alexander Wood, a linen merchant from Limerick, laid out the village with an abundance of trees, on high ground overlooking Lough Derg. In 1838, on the night of the Big Wind, Saint Brigid's church, standing beside the round tower, was badly damaged. In 1845 a small pier was erected at Mountshannon, principally for the landing of the rich marl dredged from the lake, that was once used as a fertiliser. In the 1970s the harbour was extended.

The village's Church of Ireland church is a simple gothic building associated with Saint Caimin. The Board of First Fruits gave a loan of £390 towards the building of the church. A headstone in the adjoining graveyard recalls a tragedy on 4 September 1876 when the two sons of the rector were drowned in Lough Derg.

Peaceful Mountshannon, c. 1997.

A tranquil scene in Mountshannon, c. 1996.

Church of Ireland, Mountshannon, c. 1997.

Mountshannon House is an elegant building at the northern entrance to the village. The original house, owned by the Tandy family was a one-storey building. One of the most famous members of the family was Napper Tandy (1740-1803), the United Irishman, who is believed to have built the gates while residing there in 1792. In 1798 he was leader of the French expeditionary force that landed in Donegal but retreated. In 1802 he was captured and sentenced to death but Napoleon demanded and obtained his extradition.

At the end of the nineteenth century, the main section of Mountshannon House was constructed. A later owner of the house was Lady Talbot de Malahide who, in 1956, presented it to An Oige as a youth hostel.

Like so many other villages in the locality, Mountshannon is a base for anglers. The village has the added bonus of being a first-rate sailing centre, particularly since Shannon Navigation reconstructed the old Mountshannon Harbour. The harbour has become the focus for those hiring angling boats and cruisers and as the location for the Iniscealtra Sailing Club. The village still retains many stone-built houses and decorative buildings and in 1981 Mountshannon was the national winner of the Tidy Towns Competition organised by Bord Failte.

SCARRIFF

The medium-sized town of Scarriff, south-west of Mountshannon, is conveniently situated near the shore of Scarriff Bay, one of the most attractive areas of Lough Derg.

Sailing on Lough Derg at Mountshannon, c. 1996.

The name Scarriff in Irish is An Scairbh, 'the rough shallow ford' that takes its name from an ancient ford across the Scarriff River.

In 1315 a force of Anglo-Normans was defeated by a combined force of O'Briens in the townland of Ballynahinch, close to Mountshannon. In 1543 King Henry VIII appointed Donough O'Grady Knight of Tomgraney to build a castle around which the town gradually developed.

Originally the river was navigable up to the shallows at Scarriff but only in winter when the level of the lake was high. In the 1840s the Shannon Commissioners dredged the river and increased the height of the banks and formed a harbour by closing off one side of the small island. On the northern bank, where the river enters the lake, there is a botanically-rich marshland area that contains some rare species.

In May 1842, the Scarriff workhouse was built at a cost of £6,400 and could house 600 peasants. Prior to this, many of the poor were living in hovels in totally unsanitary conditions and there was widespread death especially amongst children from cholera and malnutrition. With the outbreak of famine, the workhouse was inundated with people seeking admission and many had to be refused permission due to shortage of space. Numerous single people died from malnutrition on the outskirts around the workhouse.

In November 1880 the North Clare tenants and the Land League organised a demonstration in Scarriff and 10,000 people attended. It was proposed that they would in future refuse to pay no higher rents than dictated in Griffith's Valuation. In 1886 prices for farm produce dropped dramatically but rents were retained at the same level.

A keep tower near Scariff.

In 1887 the tenants of Colonel John O'Callaghan's large estate in Bodyke, a small village, about 3 miles west of Scarriff, appealed to him to reduce their rents but he declined. The tenants then combined effectively under the leadership of their parish priest, Fr Peter Murphy, and with the support of the National Land League refused to accept their landlord's terms. On 2 June 1887 the sheriff and his men were attacked with stones and boiling water as the tenants strongly opposed the evictions by barricading their homes. Troops and police reinforcements were called in to restore order. Finally, following a protracted struggle twenty-eight families were evicted but the people of Bodyke gained national attention and support. Michael Davitt, founder of the National Land League, addressed a huge meeting in the village. The events received widespread coverage in the Irish and British press. Over 5,000 people from around the country gathered to stand by the tenants and the unity of the tenants of Bodyke was to serve

Enjoying the sun on a doorstep in Scariff.

as an example to other areas. The matter was raised in the House of Commons and there were charges against the brutality of the police. There was a rift in the National Land League due to Charles Stewart Parnell's involvement with Katheraine O'Shea and negotiations broke down. Eventually Fr Murphy made a payment offer to Colonel O'Callaghan that was agreed and the tenants were allowed to return to their homes.

On 18 September 1919 a group of Volunteers attacked the RIC barracks in the town but the bombs failed to ignite. In 1920 Black and Tans were based in the Town Hall and created much bitterness locally.

Scarriff has always been an important market town and the old weighhouse is still preserved in the town square as a marker of its importance. The town is accessible from the lake through the River Graney and is navigable for pleasure boats and cruisers up to the harbour. This is a good coarse and game angling centre with streams containing

The weigh house, Scariff.

The quiet village of Feakle.

brown trout flowing into Scarriff Bay, most notably the River Graney, that flows from Lough Atorick through Lough Graney and Lough O'Grady. The area is reputed to be the burial place of Graney who gave her name to the river and lake, and was drowned in the latter

FEAKLE

Feakle is a secluded village on the southern slopes of the Slieve Aughty Mountains, in the remote heart of the East Clare hills, on the road from Gort to Scarriff. The name Feakle in Irish is Fiacal, 'Tooth' or 'Sharp Crag' and other sources believe that the name derived from Fia-Choill, 'the Deer Wood.' In the seventh century Saint Cuan was reputed to have founded a church here. According to legend he fell while crossing a stream, breaking a tooth. This interpretation could connect with the Fiacal name.

In the fifth century the English in south Munster crossed the River Shannon into West Thomond but were stopped by Conor and his Dalcassin force at Kilbarron near Feakle. The Irish force completely routed the English, killing most of them.

The poet Brian Merriman (1749-1805) was born in Ennistymon but lived at Lough Graney. His father worked as a stonemason and on leaving school Brian became a teacher and ran a small farm. It was there that he wrote his masterpiece 'Cuirt' an Mheadhoin Oiche (The Midnight Court), first published in 1800. Lord Longford, Arland Ussher and Frank O'Connor have since translated the poem into English. O'Connor's version of the bawdy poem was the most controversial and was banned twice by the Censorship Board. Merriman died in Limerick in 1805 and was buried in the family grave in the old graveyard at Feakle. Annually the Merriman Society holds a summer school at a Clare venue to celebrate his memory.

Close to Merriman's grave is the burial place of Biddy Early. She was christened Bridget Ellen Connors but was always referred to as Early, her mother's name. She was born in 1798 in Faha and in 1815 came to work for a doctor in Feakle. There was strong belief that she spoke to fairies and travelled the roads of Clare. She was famous for her cures and predictions but displeased the clergy. Some believed that she was a wise woman while others classed her as a witch. In 1856 she was charged with practising witchcraft but the charge was dismissed as nobody would testify against her. She married four times and in 1874 she became ill and the priest threw her magic potions into a lake. She died that same year. Her cottage has been restored and is popular with visitors. Lady Gregory assembled a good deal of the folklore relating to Biddy Early which appears in the book *Visions and Beliefs of the West of Ireland*.

Johnny Patterson was born in Feakle in 1840. He was a well-known circus clown and in characteristic Irish fashion interspersed his clowning with sentimental songs, most of which he wrote himself. In 1889 he was killed in Tralee during a political meeting.

East Clare Heritage Centre, Tuamgraney.

In September 1919 the Feakle Company of the Volunteers attacked an RIC patrol, killing and wounding a number of them.

On 10 December 1974 a historic meeting took place in Smyth's Hotel, Feakle, between the Army Council of the Provisional IRA and a group of Protestant Northern Ireland clergymen led by Revd William Arlow. The IRA realised that Arlow was informally in touch with Sir Frank Cooper, Permanent Secretary at the Northern Ireland Office. Alerted by the Northern Ireland registration plates of the clergymen's cars, the Special Branch arrived at the venue and the Provos made a hasty retreat. The IRA considered the proposals and there was a temporary cease-fire.

TUAMGRANEY

The village of Tuamgraney is about 2 miles south of Scarriff, on the R463 road. Beyond Tinarana Bay, the road runs around the shoulder of Caher Mountain (758 feet) and west to Tuamgraney. The name Tuamgraney in Irish is Tuaim Greine, 'The Tomb of Grian' or 'Graney.' The name derives from the legendary Grian, daughter of a local king who drowned in the lake.

In the seventh century Saint Cronan of Holy Island, founded a monastery at Tuamgraney. The Vikings from Limerick attacked and looted the monastery on a number of occasions. With its illuminated manuscripts and chalices it proved rich pickings for the invaders. In the tenth century Abbot Cormac O'Killeen restored the

The ruined castle in Tuamgraney.

monastery. Later Brian Boru took an interest in the monastery and is believed to have assisted the monks in rebuilding it. Up to the 1980s Saint Cronan's was utilised by the Church of Ireland for services when they presented it to the community. In 1989 it opened as the East Clare Heritage Centre.

The village was populated from the twelfth century when a small community developed around a castle of the O'Grady clan. In 1543 King Henry VIII granted Sir Denis O'Grady of Fassaghmore eleven townlands including Tuamgraney. Descendants of O'Grady built Raheen House, one of whose residents was the poet and author, S.R. Lysagh. His son, Dr Edward Lysagh, was Chief Herald of Ireland and a Senator. Shannon View House was the residence of the Reddin family who ran nearby mills and warehouses and shipped their products from Scarriff River Quay. Ballyvannon House,

The ruined castle in Tuamgraney.

The Clare writer, Edna O'Brien, with President Mary MacAleese.

the seat of Lord Dunboyne, who built it in the early eighteenth century. During the Plan of Campaign there were evictions in the area. Some of the tenant farmers fought these evictions.

The author and playwright, Edna O'Brien, was born in 1932 in Dewsboro House, between Scarriff and Tuamgraney. Her first novel, *The Country Girls*, was published in 1960 and is understood to be based on her formidable early years in the locality. Controversy surrounded the publication and the Parish Priest of Tuamgraney publicly burned a copy of the book to display his disgust. Edna O'Brien has written a number of other novels including *August is a Wicked Month*, *Girl with Green Eyes*, *Girls in their Married Bliss* and *Returning* as well as a number of screenplays, stage and radio plays.

In the village centre there is a large grotto known as the Calvary of East Clare and a memorial park in honour of those who lost their lives between 1916-22. Nearby are the woods of Raheen estate that has large primeval oak trees of great antiquity. One of these is known as Brian Boru's Tree.

There is an abundance of spectacular scenery in the environs of the village, particularly at Lough Graney, 2 miles north, framed by wooded hills. The area around the village has a number of small lakes that offer excellent fishing. For a small place, Tuamgraney is a hive of activity during the festival in August. Within a short distance

Ruined old church in Tulla.

Old houses in Tulla.

of the village there are three gallery stones known as Tobergrania, Altoir Ultach and Dermot and Grania's Bed. There was once a well at Tobergrania that reputedly had curative powers.

TULLA

Tulla is a small village situated on high ground, 9 miles east of Ennis. The name Tulla in Irish is Tulac, 'A Little Hill.' In the early fourteenth century the area was divided into Tulla Upper and Tulla Lower and was controlled by the MacNamaras.

The highest point in the area is Maghera Mountain. North of Tulla is Asalpnagown, with excellent forest walks. West of the village is Cullane Wood in the grounds of Cullane House. Within a short distance is the old demesne of Kiltanan. Close to the estate there is an underground stream and some limestone caves called 'The Toumeens'. Two miles west in Milltown is Dermot and Grania's Bed, the only remaining pre-historic chamber tombs in this townland. Within the environs of Tulla there are a number of O'Brien and MacMahon castles. There are also the ruins of a medieval parish church and a barrel-vaulted seventeenth-century church.

In the village there are the remains of Saint Moculla's medieval parish church, believed to have been founded in the seventh century. In 1846, due to the high level of poverty in the district, the Poor Law Union built a workhouse. The usual strict rules applied and only families were admitted. Males and females lived in separate quarters

Sixmilebridge in festive mood, c. 1996.

and no single people were admitted. They had to fend for themselves on the outside and try to get a place on a relief scheme.

In July 1852, during polling in the election, friction arose between the landlords and their angry tenants. The central figure was the Tory candidate, Colonel Crofton Moore Vandeleur. Many of the tenants were still angry with him for his treatment of peasants during the famine. On polling day at Tulla troops were drafted in as locals attempted to prevent freeholding tenants voting for Vandeleur. The situation became so tense that a magistrate ordered the troops to open fire on the protesters but the clergy intervened and a compromise was reached.

In the 1850s it is believed that Biddy Early, thought by some to have been a witch for her healing powers, worked at Affick House, as a parlour maid for the Spaight family.

Tulla is also a noted fishing centre and known as the Clare Lakelands, with a number of small lakes ringing the village.

Traditional music features strongly in the area and the Tulla Ceili Band is one of the best known ceili bands in the country. Local musicians came together and formed the band in 1946. They have made several successful tours abroad to Irish venues in the United States and England. In the 1960s there was a dip in their popularity but the set dancing revival brought them back in demand. Their signature tune is 'The Humours of Tulla'.

SIXMILEBRIDGE

The picture postcard village of Sixmilebridge is on the road north-west of the Shannon and at the foot of Woodcock Hill. The name Sixmilebridge in Irish is Droichead Abhann O gCearnaigh, 'Bridge of the Ogarney River.'

The hilly main street with its colourful shops, pubs and business premises, runs up from the attractive old bridge.

The original small village, on the Tulla–Limerick road that began around the river, grew at the beginning of the eighteenth century when an iron-works began operating in the area. Workers and their families were attracted to the district to find work and new houses were built to cope with the influx of workers. The names of its streets indicate its Hanoverian influence and were called Hanover, Orange and George. There are some fine castles and big houses within the vicinity of Sixmilebridge. Two miles north-west is Ballycullen Castle, built in 1641 by Thomas Fanning. West of the village is Rathmore House, a late nineteenth-century two-storey house. Rath Mor, a ring fort, is in the grounds and the smaller Rath Beag is nearby. Mount Ievers is a fine Georgian house, built in 1736 for the Ievers family by John Isaac Rothery. At the end of the nineteenth century, Thomas Cregan, a magistrate for County Clare, lived at Ardcregan House in the village. In 1813 Fr Cornelius Clune built the Catholic church.

Two miles north of Sixmilebridge are the ruins of Ballymulcashel (Mountcashel) Castle, built by Conor na Srona, King of Thomond in the late fifteenth century. Five

A peaceful Sixmilebridge, c. 1996.

miles north-west in the townland of Finlough, is Tomfinlough, the site of a monastic settlement of around 550, founded by Saint Luchtighern Moccu Tratho. The remains include an early church, the gable of a small oratory and a holy well.

From 1784 trade in the locality was to be seriously affected when Henry D'Esterre constructed a toll bridge. There was a huge reduction in the number of vessels prepared to pay the charge and many avoided the area.

In July 1852 feelings were running high with the pending election and a background of evictions and rackrents. In Sixmilebridge there was fear for the safety of the free holders (who were responsible for evictions and demolishing houses) en route to the polls and an escort of soldiers was provided for them. About forty freeholding tenants from Meelick, the remaining ones on the Marquis of Conyngham's estate, were under the control of the land agent. They were under strict instructions to vote for the notorious Colonel Vandeleur. Local people turned out in large numbers to vent their anger and physically prevent them from voting. They threw stones and missiles at the freeholders in carts as they entered the village. Chaos broke out and without orders the troops opened fire and six local men were shot dead. In the confusion that followed the agent hustled a group of the Meelick voters in to vote for Vandeleur. Following the deaths, anti-landlord feelings intensified throughout the county and further attacks were waged on the supporters of Vandeleur. In the subsequent trial, eight troops were found guilty of murder but were all later acquitted.

In 1919 a leading timber merchant, James O'Regan, revived the monthly fairs in the village bringing increased trade to the district. He later purchased the Old Ground Hotel in Ennis.

In May 1919 a force of Volunteers attacked the RIC barracks in Sixmilebridge. On 20 January 1920 some Volunteers laid an ambush at Glenwood, on the road between Sixmilebridge and Broadford, on a Black and Tan patrol. Six of the Tans were shot dead. In retaliation the British set fire to over thirty houses in the locality.

In 1995 three players from the village had the privilege of playing on the successful Clare team that won their first All-Ireland Senior Hurling Final in Croke Park since 1914.

In the summer of 1996 St Ievers House in Sixmilebridge, was chosen as the principal location for the feature film, *Serpent's Kiss*, a tale of intrigue and deceit set in Gloucestershire in 1699. The £11 million production starred Greta Scacchi, Pete Postlethwaite, Richard E. Grant and Ewan McGregor and was directed by cinematographer Philippe Rousselot, making his directorial debut. The lavish production gave employment locally to craftsmen and villagers who worked as extras.

O'BRIENBRIDGE

The small, pretty village of O'Brienbridge is situated on the road from Limerick to Killaloe, on the western shore of Lough Derg. This was one of the most important fording places on the River Shannon. In 1506 Turlough O'Brien and the Bishop of Killaloe erected the original bridge here but in 1536 Lord Grey destroyed it. In 1651, Colonel Ireton and a Cromwellian army forced a passage of the River Shannon at this juncture.

The residents of O'Brienbridge take great pride in their village, with buildings colourfully painted and the village green landscaped and adorned with a grotto. The village is beautifully located beside the river where visitors can try their hand at coarse fishing or enjoy a leisurely stroll. Appropriately there are two bridges, the old structure over the river and a more recent construction spanning the canal. O'Brienbridge is the only crossing of the Shannon between Killaloe and Limerick.

The building of a large reservoir by the Shannon Electricity Scheme involved the rising of the river level to that of the lake and the creation of a weir. The bulk of the water is diverted into the canal to be utilised at the hydroelectric works at Ardnacrusha, 4 miles west. The remainder of the flow follows the old course of the Shannon past the Falls of Coonass and the fishing village of Castleconnell. Subsequently it became impossible for high-masted vessels to pass under the bridge until in 1929 a new swivel bridge replaced one of the stone arches making navigation possible again.

In September 1920 during an exchange between a force of Volunteers and RIC men, two constables were shot dead in O'Brienbridge.

KILLALOE

The town of Killaloe is situated beside the Clare/Tipperary border that runs down the centre of the River Shannon. The town is charmingly located on the west bank of the river where it emerges from Lough Derg and makes its way through the gap between Slieve Bernagh and the Atta Mountains. Killaloe, a designated Heritage Town, is linked to Ballina in County Tipperary by a thirteen arch bridge. In the early eleventh century the first bridge over the river was a wooden structure. In later years the crossing was protected by a MacNamara castle on the Killaloe side and an O'Brien castle at Ballina. The name Killaloe in Irish is Cill-Dha-Lua, 'the Church of Saint Lua' who was the first bishop of Killaloe in the sixth century.

In the ninth century a large church of the same name was erected on the site. Up to 1929 it stood on Saint Friar's Island, just below the bridge but was transferred stone by stone to its present site when the hydroelectric scheme raised the level of the water, submerging the island. The great artificial dam of the Shannon Hydro Electric Works, has superseded the national dam of the Gorge of Killaloe. About one mile outside Killaloe is Crag Liath or Crag Fort (also known as Greenaun), above the road north to Scarriff.

The Dalcassian stronghold of Kincora was located on a hill overlooking the river. This was a strategic position from which residents were able to withstand Viking raids during the tenth century. Under the patronage of various Dalcassian kings Killaloe developed into an important location of religious life. This was also the location of the palace of Kincora, the great stronghold of Brian Boru. Kincora was a royal residence for over two centuries before the reign of Brian Boru and remained so for another century after his death. At another period, Boru's base was on the site of the present Catholic church.

Brian Boru was born in 941 to Cinnaide and Be Bhionn, members of the Dal gCais family – known as the Dalcassians – then the rulers of the kingdom of Thomond, representing the area of Clare. The exact place of his birth is uncertain but is strongly believed to be on the County Clare shore of Lough Derg, possibly at the fortress of Ceann Coraidh, anglicised to Kincora, north of the present Killaloe.

Brian Boru held court in Kincora from where he went on frequent hunting expeditions into the forests of Munster and presided over vast banquets of game, Danish ale and Irish heather wine. A one-mile-long, covered passage extended from Kincora to 'the Green fort beside the lordly Shannon' where the warrior guests were housed.

Brian made it obligatory that everybody was to have a surname. His own descendants chose his name as a form of their own. This was to firmly establish the name O'Brien as a formidable name in the history of County Clare for many centuries. It is reputed

Killaloe and St Flannan's Cathedral on the River Shannon, c. 1998.

St Flannan's Cathedral, Killaloe, 2004.

that Brian Boru was married four times and his offspring formed branches of the O'Brien clan.

Brian saw the potential of the Shannon for a method of control. He was the first king to establish a navy, as it was possible to sail up to Carrick-on-Shannon after the boats had been carried overland at the Ardnacrusha Falls. He was to build up a force of 300 ships on Lough Derg, near his base at Kincora, with which he was able to control the lower Shannon.

Brian Boru, the youngest son of the King of Thomond, was not born to greatness. He became leader of a small force, holding out in Clare against the Vikings of Limerick, that brought him to prominence with his own people. The murder of his

Graveyard in St Flannan's Cathedral, Killaloe, 2004.

eldest surviving brother, Mathghamhain, gave him the thrones of Thomond and later Munster. In 999 in the Battle of Glen Mama Brian defeated the King of Leinster and the Vikings of Dublin. With Brian's growing power base he forced the surrender of the Viking, Mael Sechnaill at Tara. Brian then replaced Ui Neill on the high throne of Ireland and was High King of Ireland from 1002 to 1014.

In 1014 Brian launched a raid into the land of Cineal gConaill in Ulster, and took the local king hostage and brought him back to Kincora. Brian's strongest opposition came from Mael Morda, king of Leinster. Morda joined with a huge force of Vikings in a show of strength with ships and horsemen at Clontarf on 23 April 1014. Brian Boru marched on Dublin on that Good Friday and so began the pitched battle that became known as 'the Battle of Clontarf.' The Irish won a decisive victory, greatly weakening the power of the Vikings in Ireland.

It is reputed that Aoibhill, the renowned banshee of the Dalcassins, appeared to Brian Boru on the eve of the Battle of Clontarf and informed him that he would be slain the following day, though not in the battle. This in fact occurred and following the victorious battle the Viking, Broder killed Brian Boru in his tent. Brian's son was also killed at that time

Mac Liag, Brian Boru's chief bard wrote the following of him (translated into English by James Clarence Mangan):

St Flannan's Oratory, Killaloe, 2004.

Oh where, Kincora, is Brian the Great?
And where is the beauty that once was thine?
Oh, where are the princes and nobles that sate
At the feast in thy halls and drank the red wines
Where, oh, Kincora?

Killaloe is steeped in ecclesiastical history. Early in the twelfth century the extent of the Diocese of Killaloe was defined. The boundary stretched from Loop Head on the Atlantic coast to Borris-in-Ossory in the Midlands and embraced County Clare, North Tipperary and parts of Counties Laois, Offaly and Limerick. The first Dean of Killaloe, elected in April 1253, was Isaac Ua Cormacain. Donal Mor O'Brien, King of Munster, was requested to build a number of cathedrals and churches in the diocese.

Cruising on the river Shannon at Killaloe, c. 1985.

Bridge over the river Shannon at Killaloe, 2004.

A traditional old shop front in Killaloe, 2004.

Another important saint associated with Killaloe is Flannan who was a bishop here in around 640. His brother, Mahon, was king of the Dalglais. In 1161 Donnchadha O'Brien, son of Murtagh Mor, became the first O'Brien bishop of Killaloe. The building of Saint Flannan's Cathedral was begun about 1180 by Donal Mor O'Brien, believed to be on the site of an earlier church. In 1185 the building was attacked by Cathal Carrach of Connacht. In the early thirteenth century the present structure was erected in a Gothic design with pointed arches. The Romanesque doorway from the earlier building was incorporated into the new structure. At the time of the reformation the cathedral changed from being Roman Catholic to Protestant. In 1276 the Norman knight, Thomas de Clare, youngest brother of the Earl of Gloucester, captured Killaloe.

In 1690 Patrick Sarsfield and his men on their famous night ride from Limerick to intercept the Williamite siege at Ballyneety, had to cross the ford at Killaloe as the bridge was heavily guarded. Sarsfield was successful and destroyed the Williamite powder supply.

In the early 1800s, faction fighting was a familiar happening in the Killaloe area. On 21 April 1829, following a fair in Killaloe, a fight broke out between the Corbans and the Hourigans in which cudgels, pitchforks and assorted weapons were used. Troops attempted to stop the fighting and fired into the crowd and shot three men dead. All were small farmers.

Robert Fowler, Church of Ireland Bishop of Killaloe and Clonfert built Clarisford House between 1771-1779, at the only ford across the Shannon from Tipperary.

The building became the Episcopal Palace until 1977 and many prominent bishops including Charles Lindsay and Richard Mant resided there.

In the early part of the twentieth century the Shannon Development Company opened a regular steamboat service between Killaloe, Athlone and Carrick-on-Shannon bringing many tourists to the area. Around this time the Duke of York (later King George V) visited Killaloe. In the intervening years many other ferry services operated from Killaloe

In 1899 the Shannon Development Company built the Lakeside Hotel. In 1916 the hotel was commandeered by British troops as a barracks giving them total access to the river crossing. Other hotels close to the bridge were also occupied by British troops during this period. In 1922 the Lakeside Hotel was destroyed by Irregulars but was rebuilt a decade later.

In November 1920 a group of Auxiliaries travelled up Lough Derg in a boat and apprehended four members of the East Clare Flying Column, Alfie Rogers, Martin Kildea, Michael Egan and Michael MacMahon in a house in Mountshannon. They brought the men back to the bridge in Killaloe, tied their hands behind their backs and shot them dead. The British authorities issued a statement stating that 'four men were shot trying to escape.'

The town is a favourite fishing centre for Lough Derg and offers many marine activities from cruising and sailing to water-skiing. Boats can be hired on the quayside. In the summer months a river bus runs pleasure cruises along the lough. Killaloe Sailing Club and Shannonside Centre are based nearby. Lough Derg, 25 miles long and up to 3 miles wide, is the largest and most southerly of the Shannon Lakes. Its contrasting course with deep indented shores and hilly background, gives it a majestic appearance. The comedian, Brendan Grace runs a pub in the village and a recent addition to the amenities is an interpretative centre and tourist office.

Other titles published by Tempus

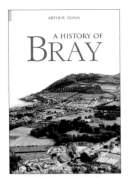

A History of Bray
ARTHUR FLYNN

This comprehensive volume recalls some of the events that have occurred in the town of Bray in County Wicklow: from smuggling in the eighteenth century and the transformation of Bray into a garrison town during the war years, to the opening of Ardmore Studios and the building of industrial estates during the 1950s and '60s. It also describes the life of the people who have lived, worked and visited the area over the centuries.
0 7524 3269 0

A History of the Black Death in Ireland
MARIA KELLY

Transported by rats and fleas in the trading vessels plying between Ireland, England and France, the plague appeared in Dublin and Drogheda in the summer of 1348. It spread quickly and virulently, reaching south towards Waterford, Youghal, Cork and Limerick and wiping out whole communities in its path. Maria Kelly goes in search of the 'Great Pestilence' whose consequences are often obscured by the intricate and tumultuous history of the time, and traces how the Irish reacted to this seemingly invisible killer.
0 7524 3185 4

Battle of the Boyne
PÁDRAIG LENIHAN

A startling history of the largest and most famous battle in Irish history, incorporating findings of a series of newly discovered sources. Was the Boyne really as important as William of Orange's propagandists claimed, or was it, as the losers – the French and many of the Irish – insisted, 'only a skirmish'? Pádraig Lenihan reconciles the political potency of the Boyne with its military indecisiveness, challenging the conventional view of this most controversial event.
0 7524 3304 0

Festival Gold Forty Years of Cheltenham Racing
STEWART PETERS

The Cheltenham Festival features the very best horses competing in the best races. It's where legends of the sport have been established, including greats such as Mill House, Arkle and Desert Orchid. Illustrated throughout with photographs from Bernard Parkin, the official Cheltenham course photographer, Festival Gold is a comprehensive history of one of racing's most exciting events.
0 7524 3287 7

If you are interested in purchasing other books published by Tempus, or in case you have difficulty finding any Tempus books in your local bookshop, you can also place orders directly through our website

www.tempus-publishing.com